EXOTIC INDIA

A Colouring Book
for relaxation and rejuvenation

Cassie Haywood

ISBN: 978-0-9944431-0-6

A CIP record for this book is available from the National Library of Australia

EXOTIC INDIA

The design of patterns, symbols, and mandalas are intrinsic to Indian identity, heritage, and hence part of everyday life. Indian design is found everywhere from objects to artefacts, fabrics and surroundings. India offers an abundance of exotic beauty and creativity at every turn, reflecting the vitality of the people and their environment.

In this book you will find 50 illustrations inspired by India. Simply choose a design which appeals to you, take a few deep breaths and start colouring. There are no rules to follow, you choose the medium and colours which speak to you. These designs open the way for letting go and inner peace, therefore allowing relaxation and rejuvenation to become part of your everyday life.

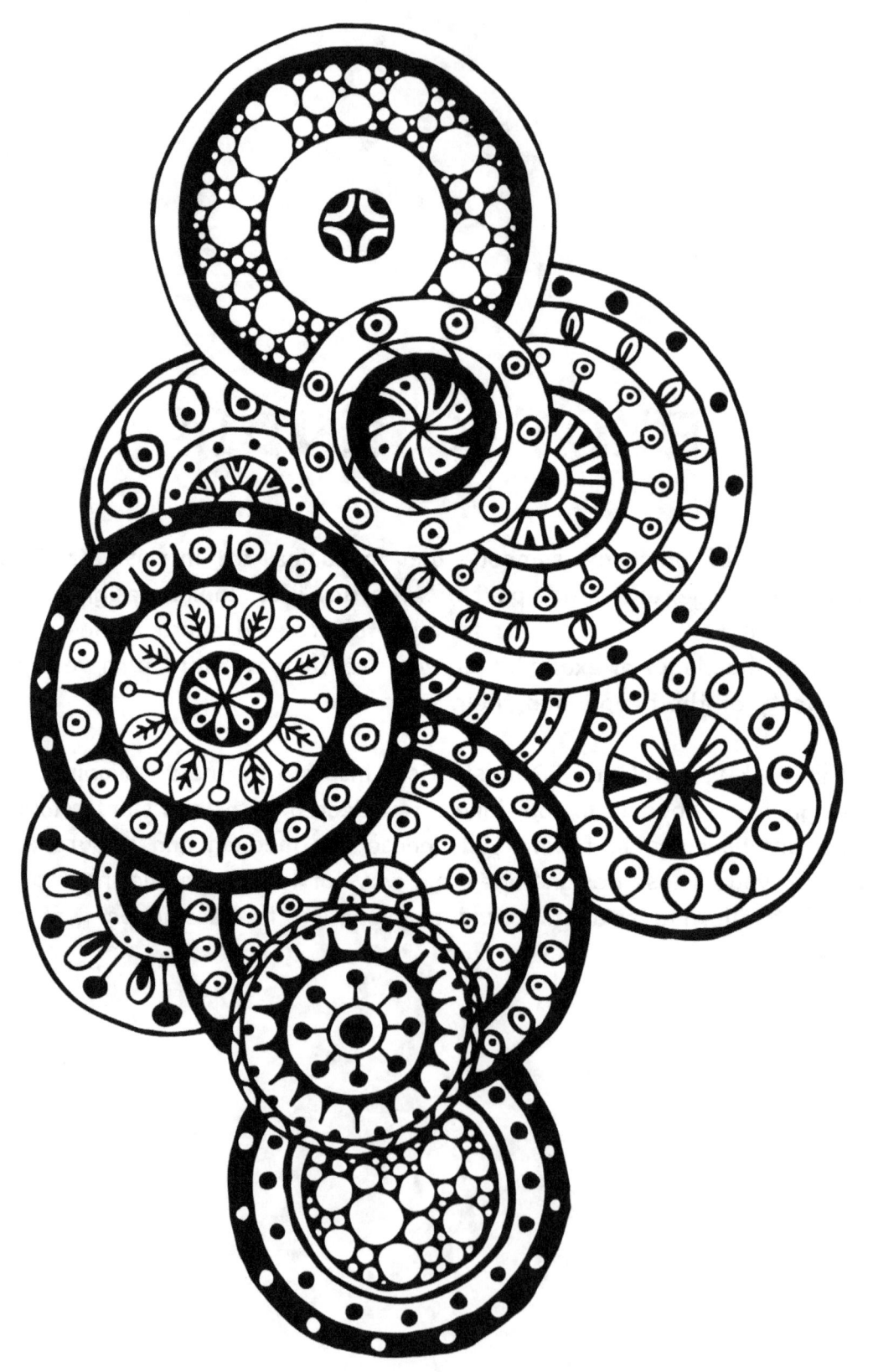

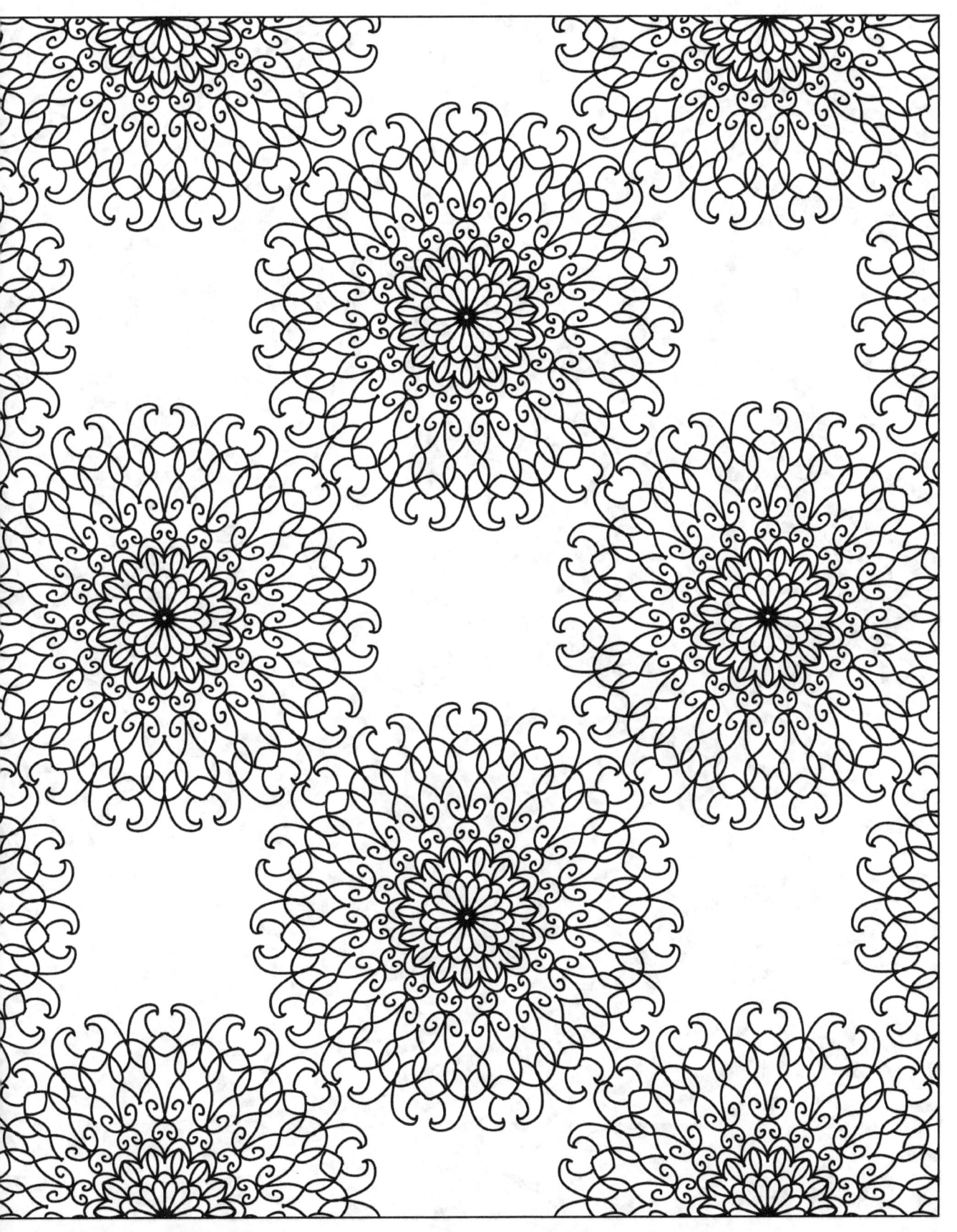

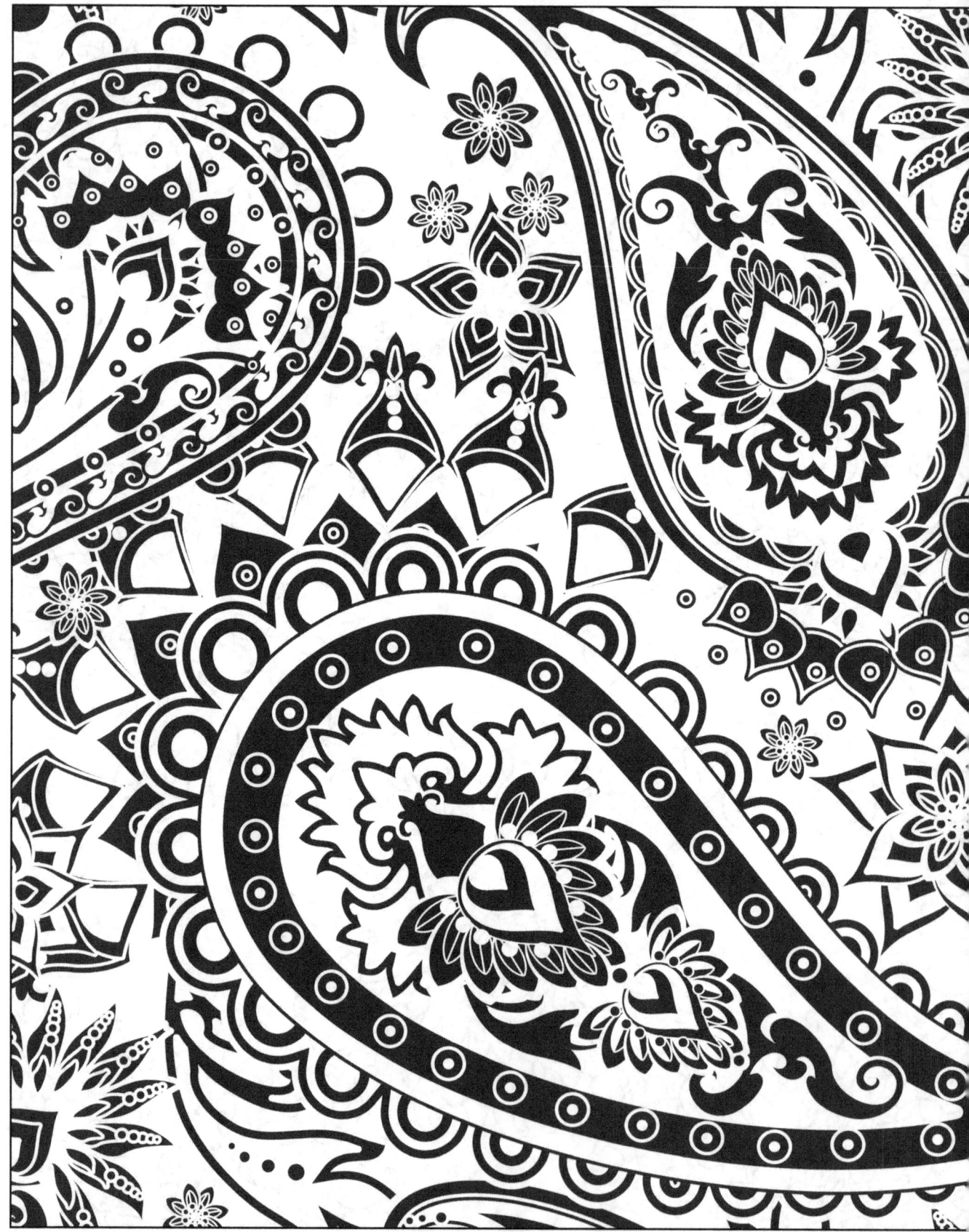

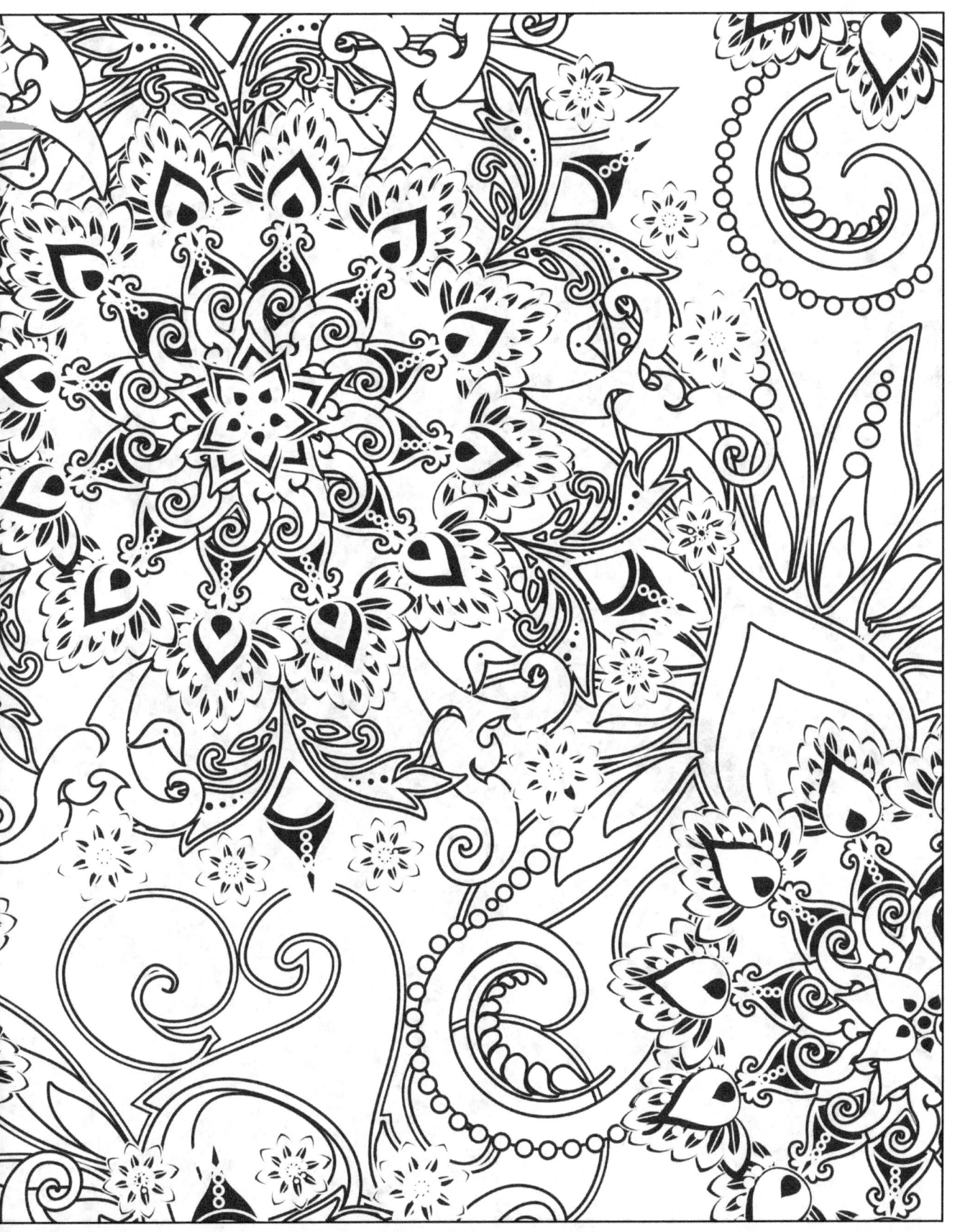

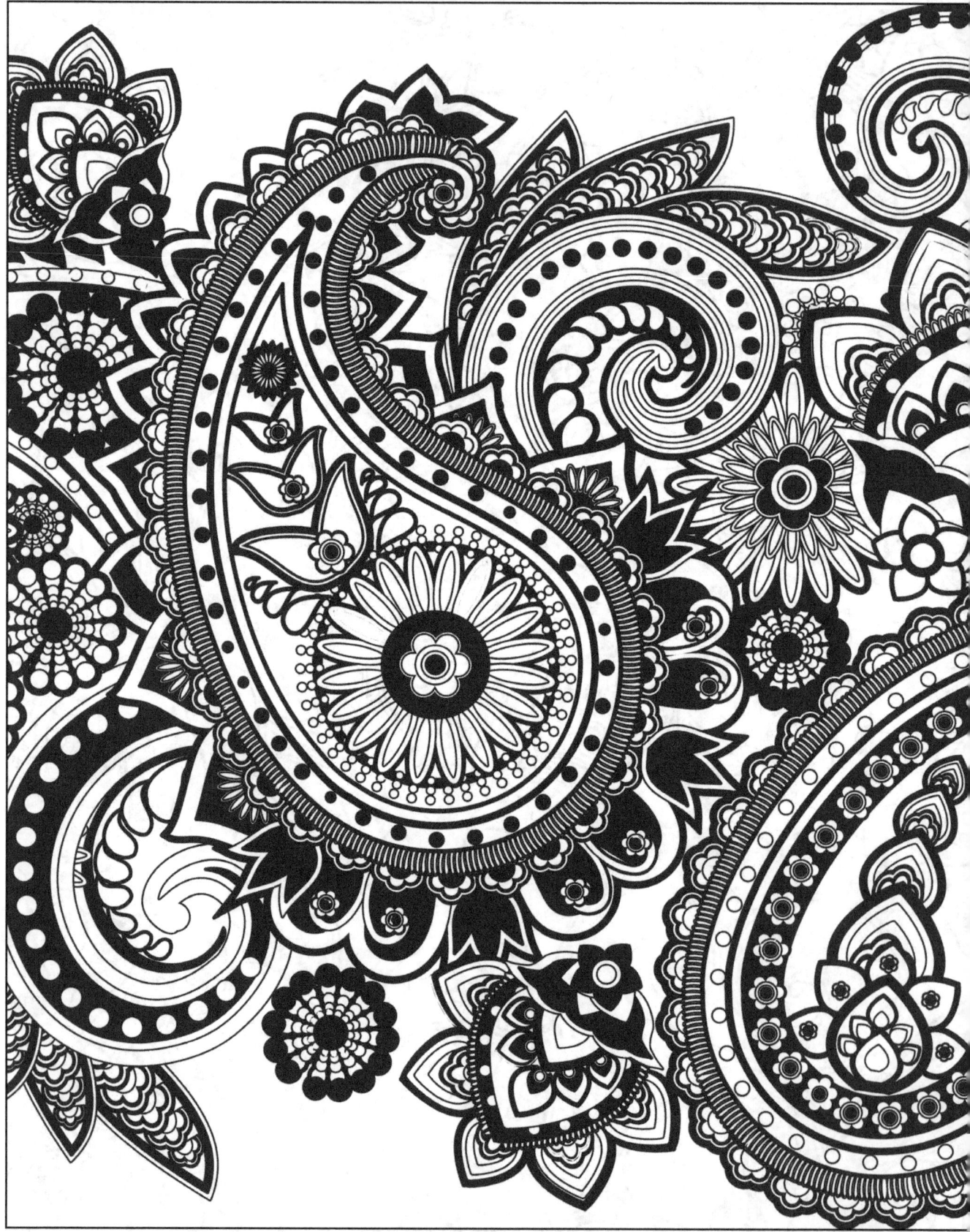

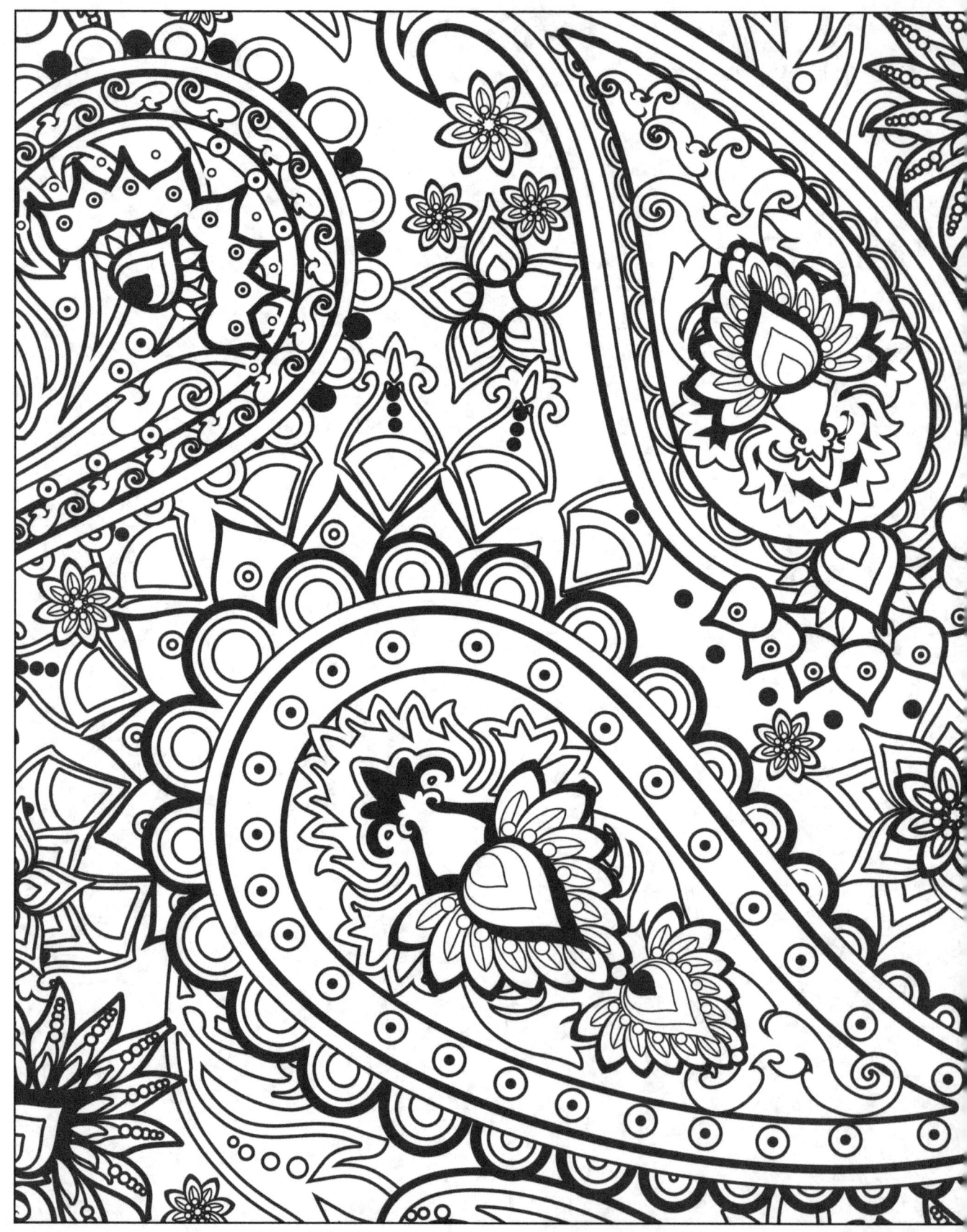

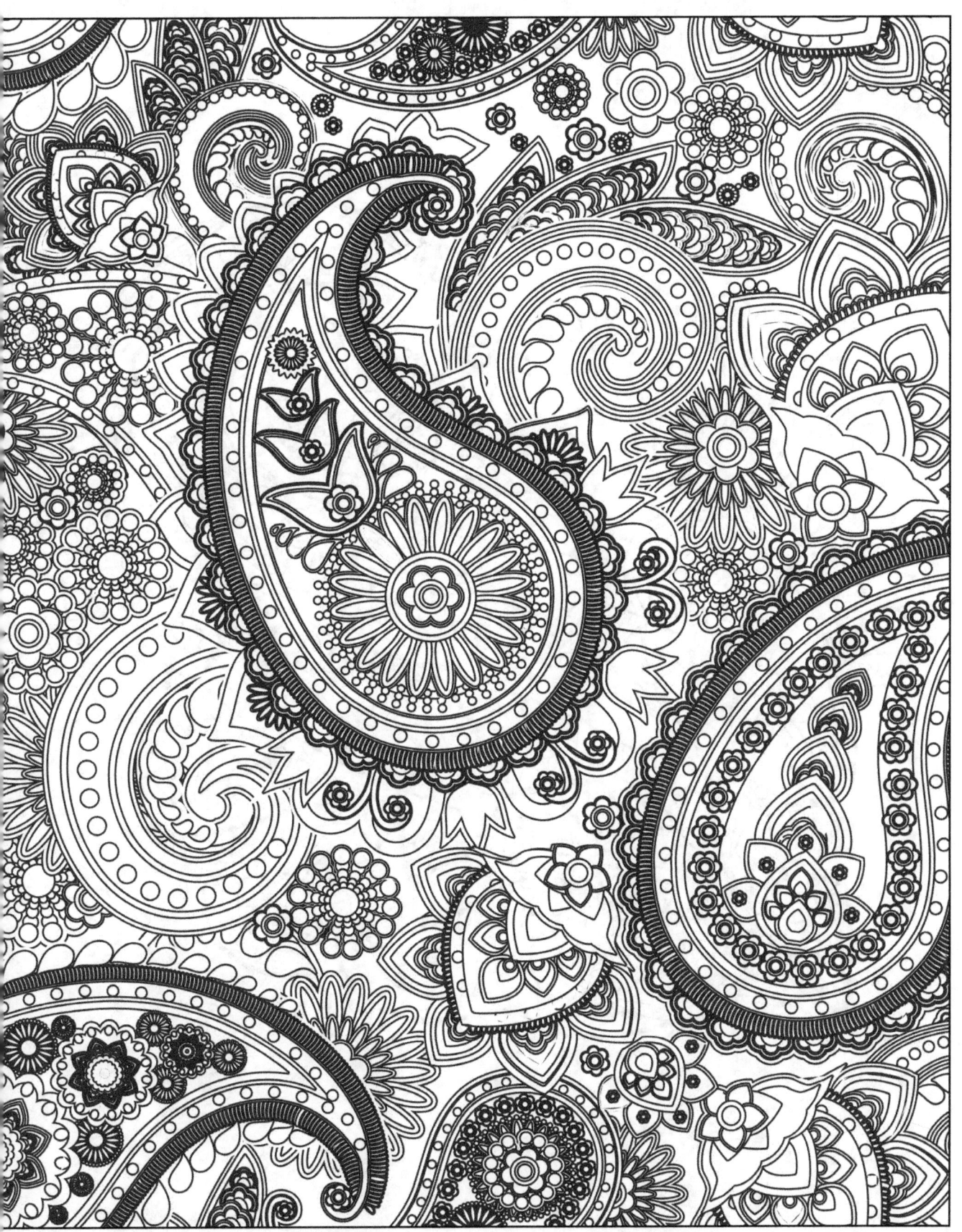

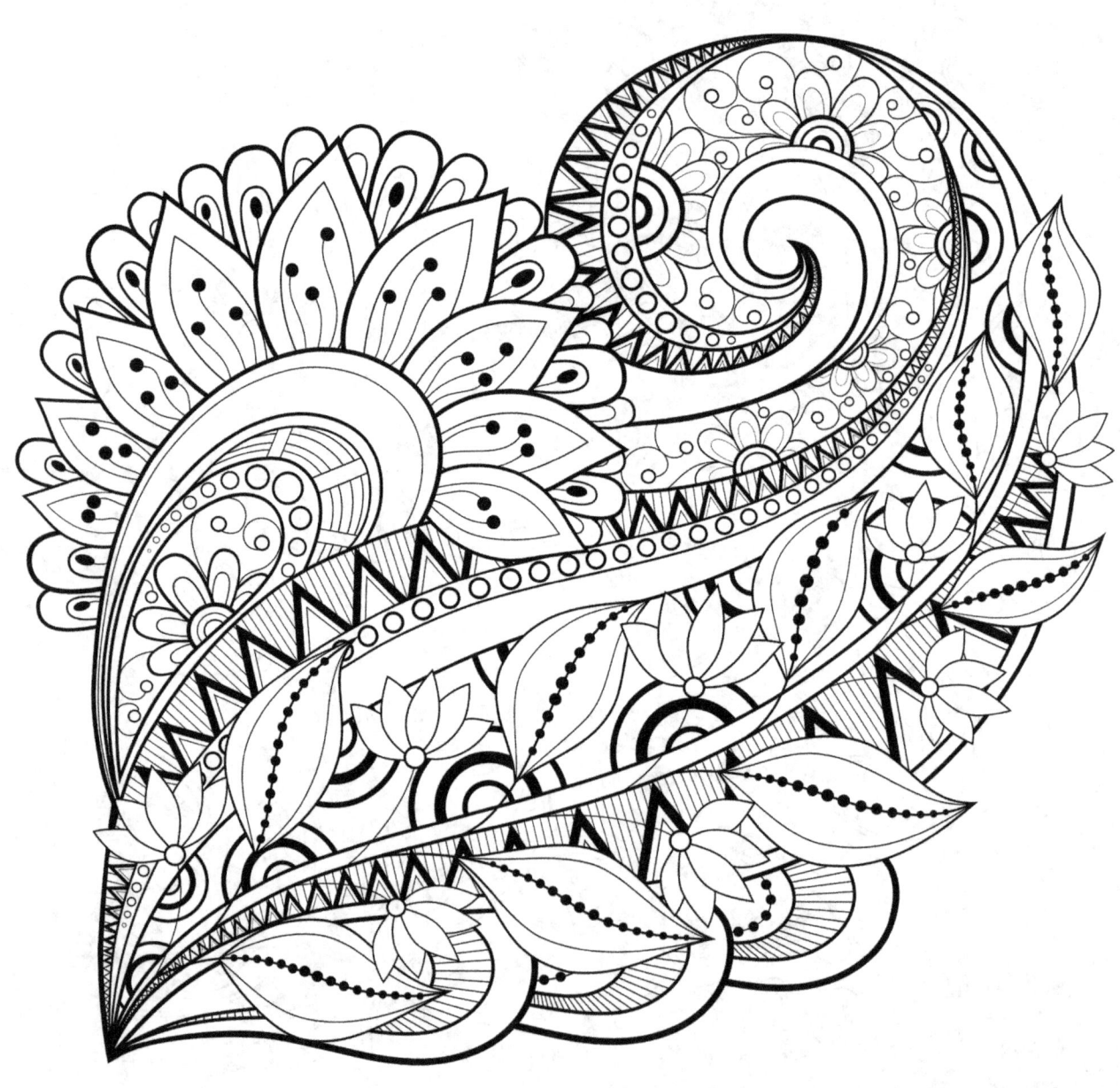

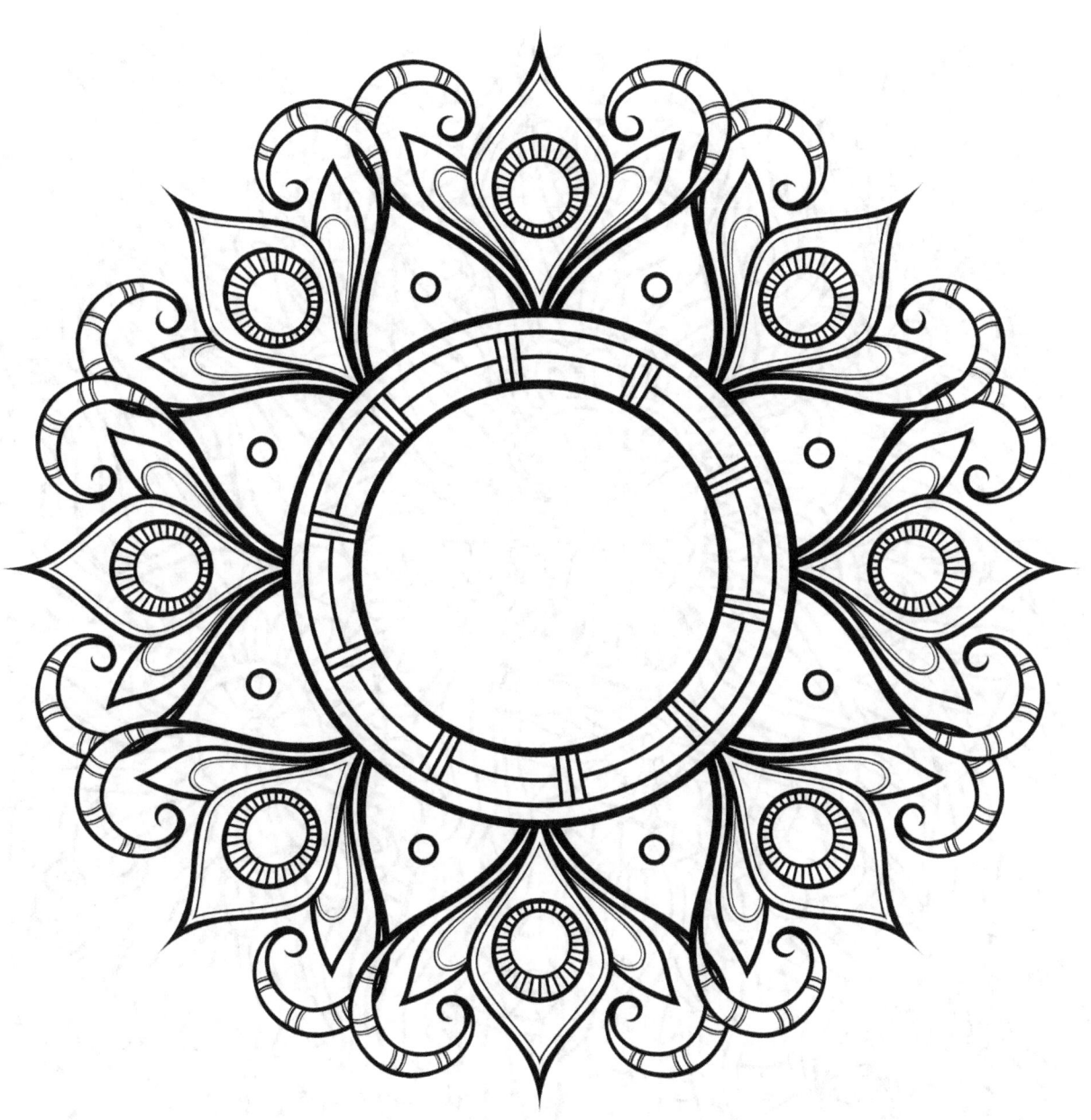

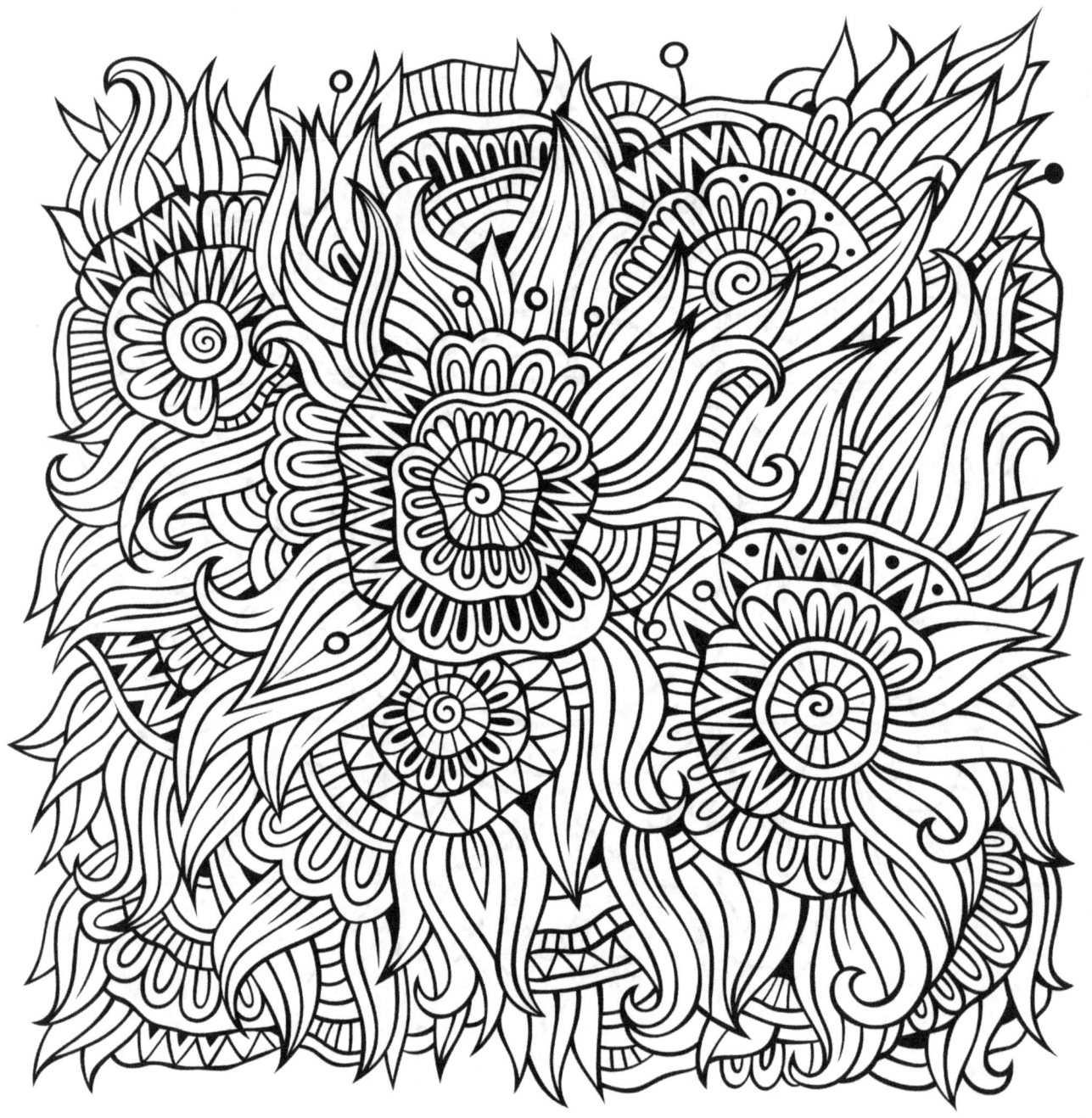

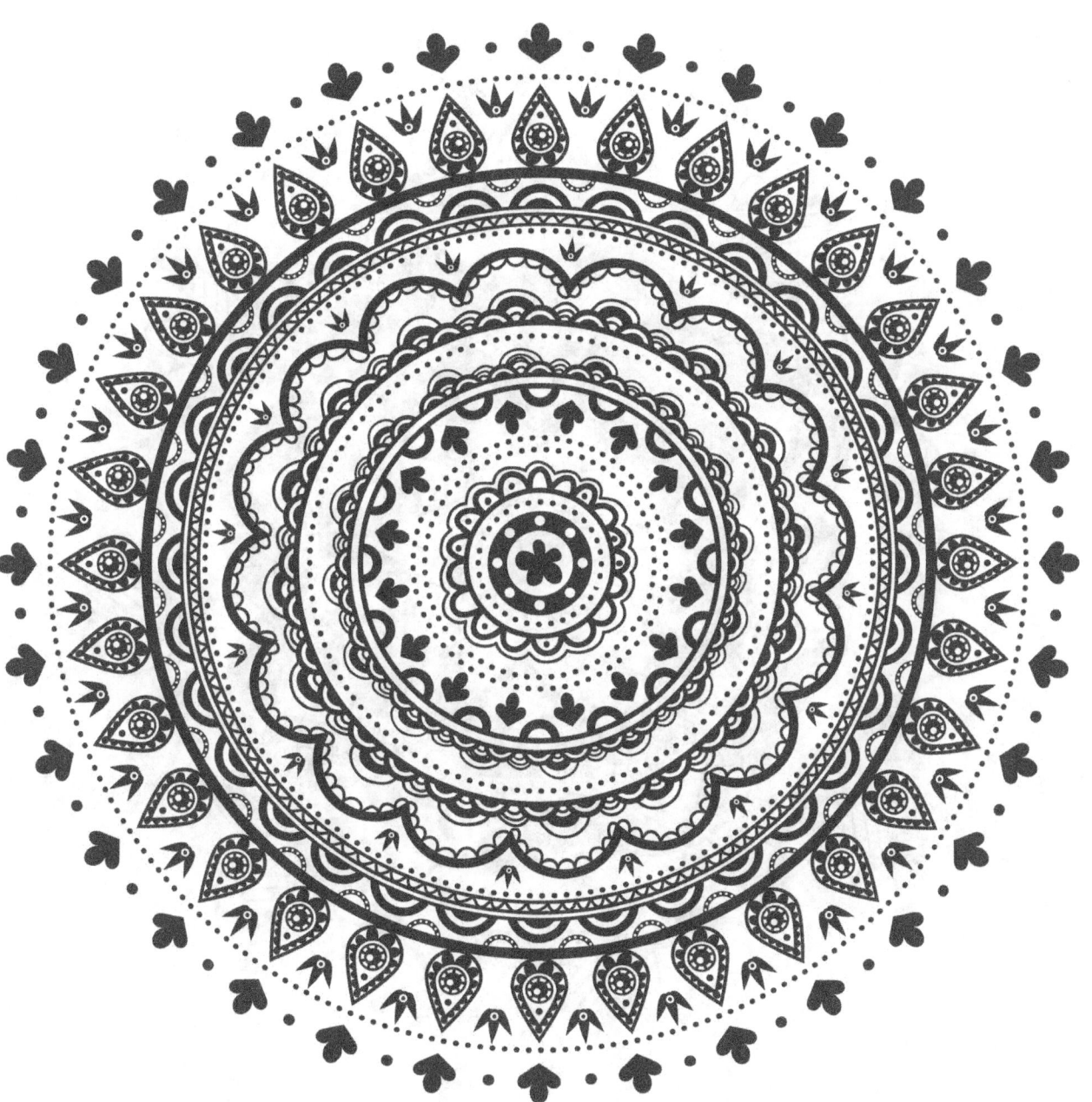

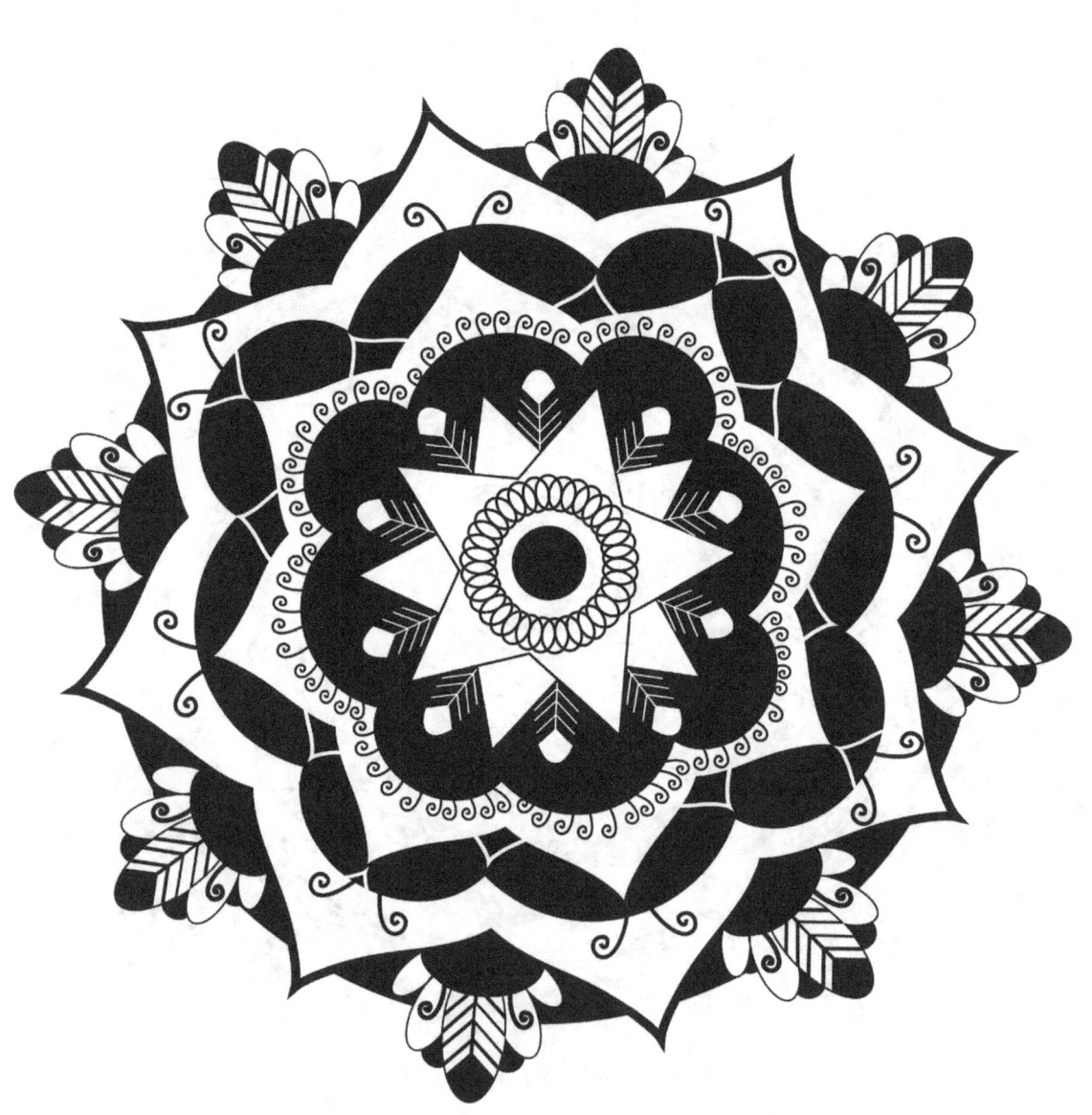

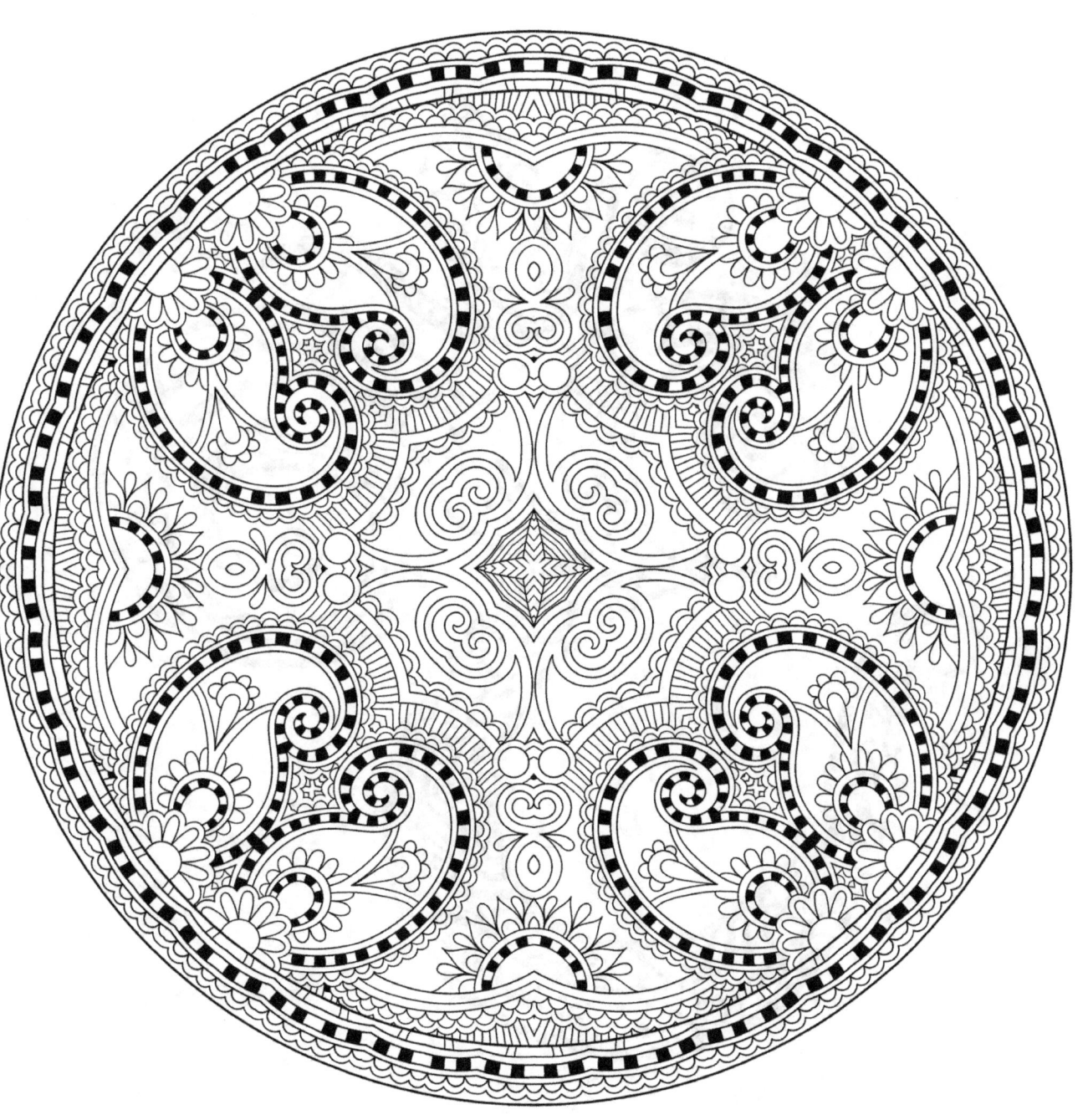

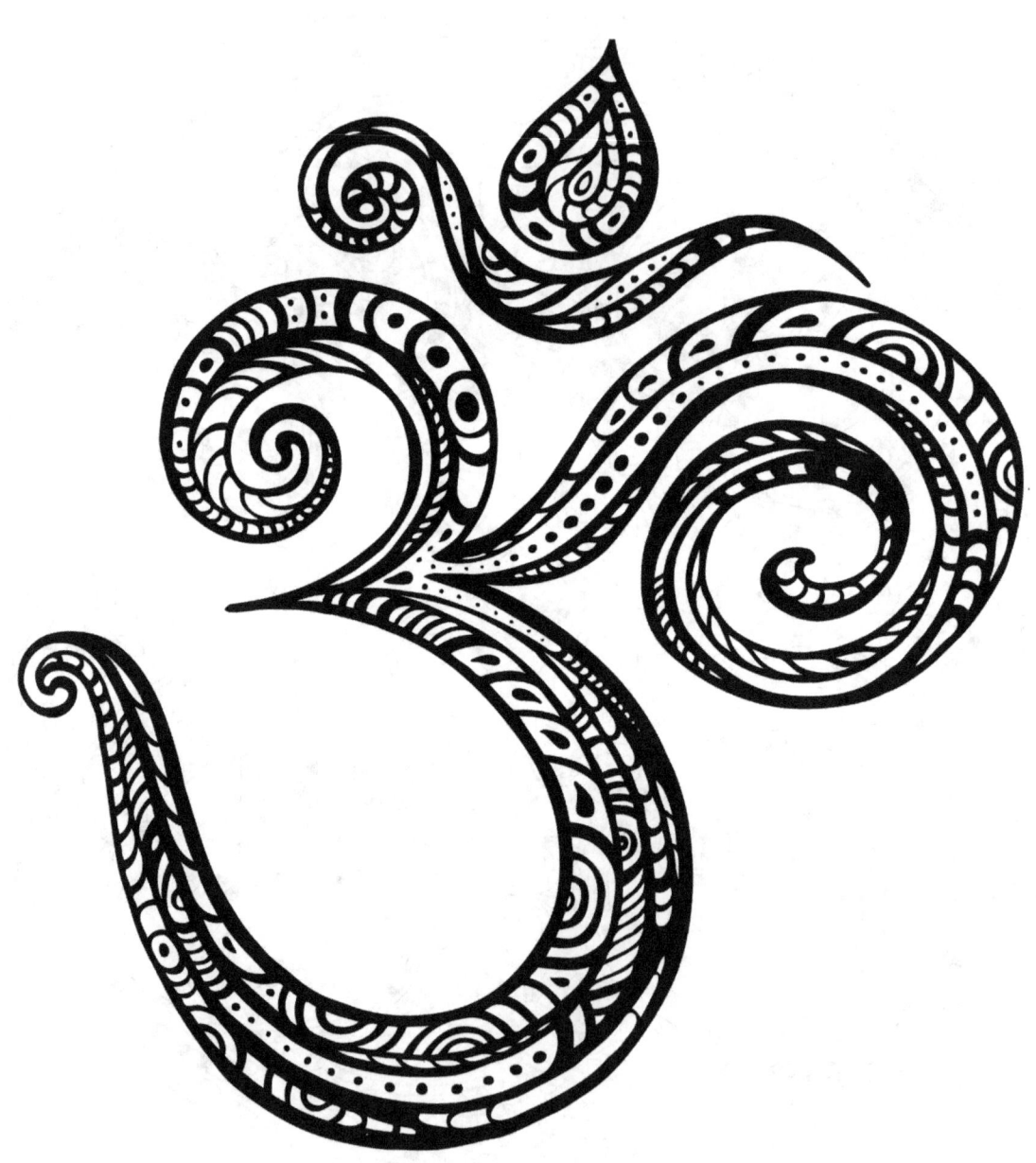

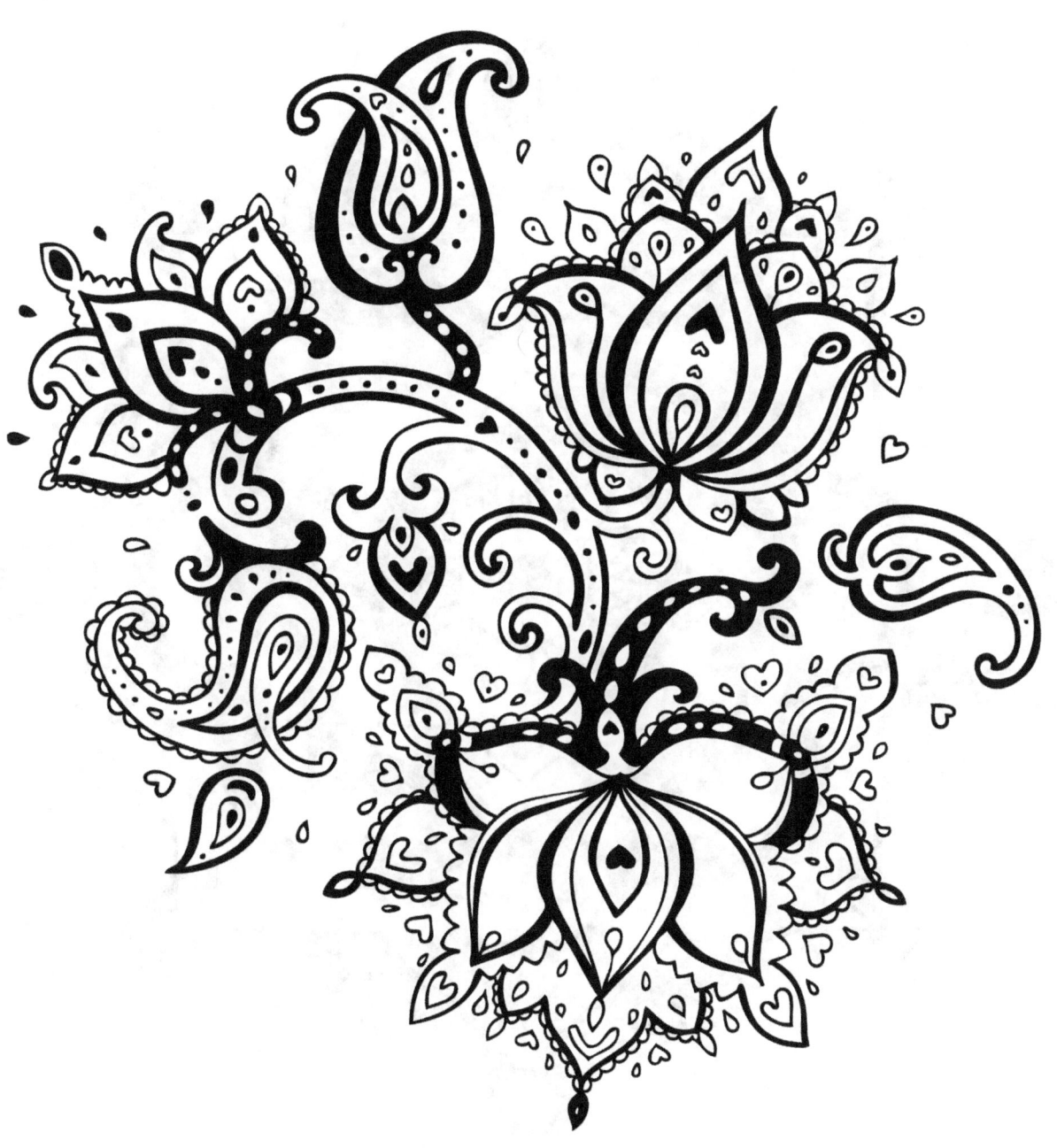

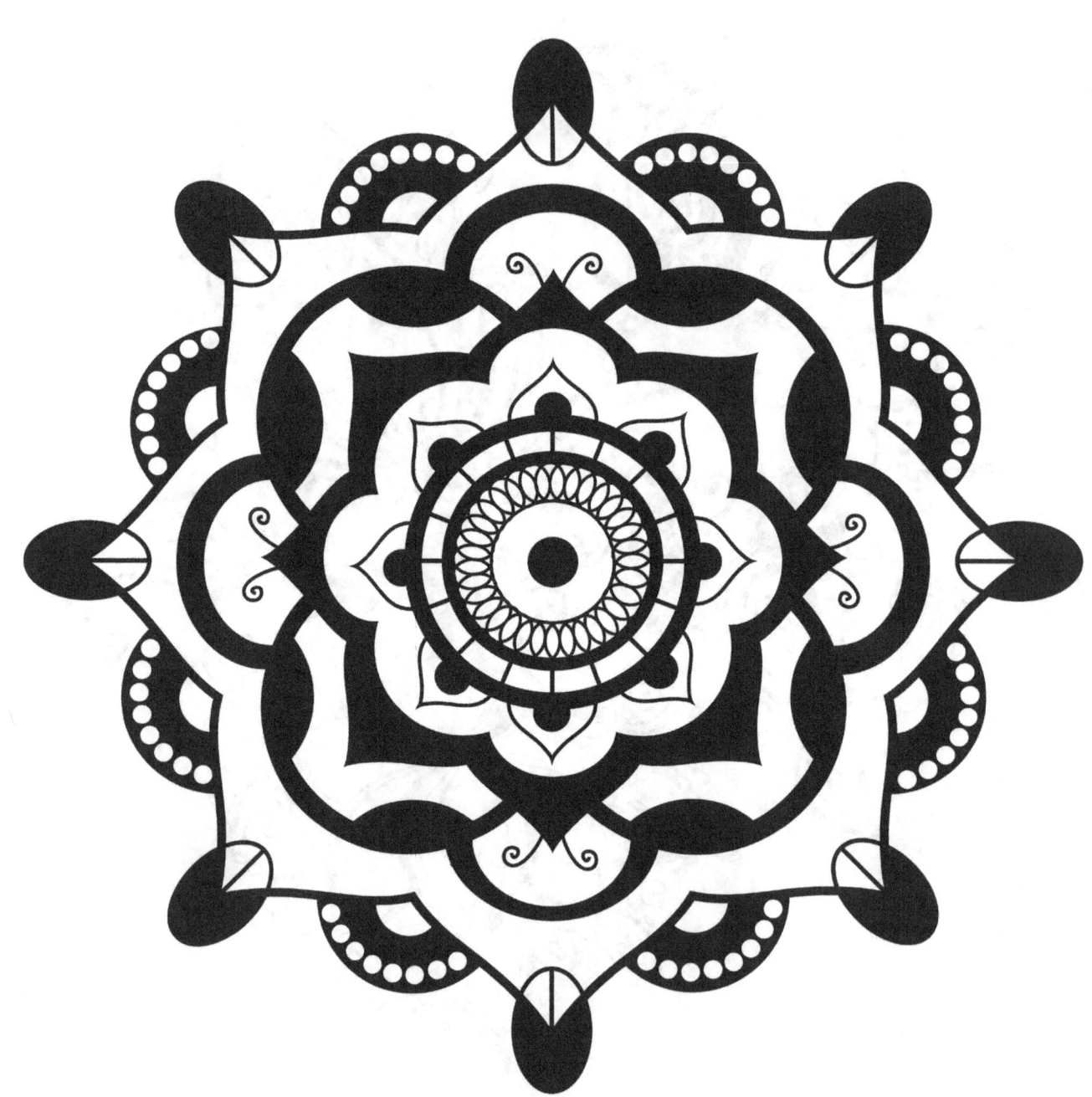

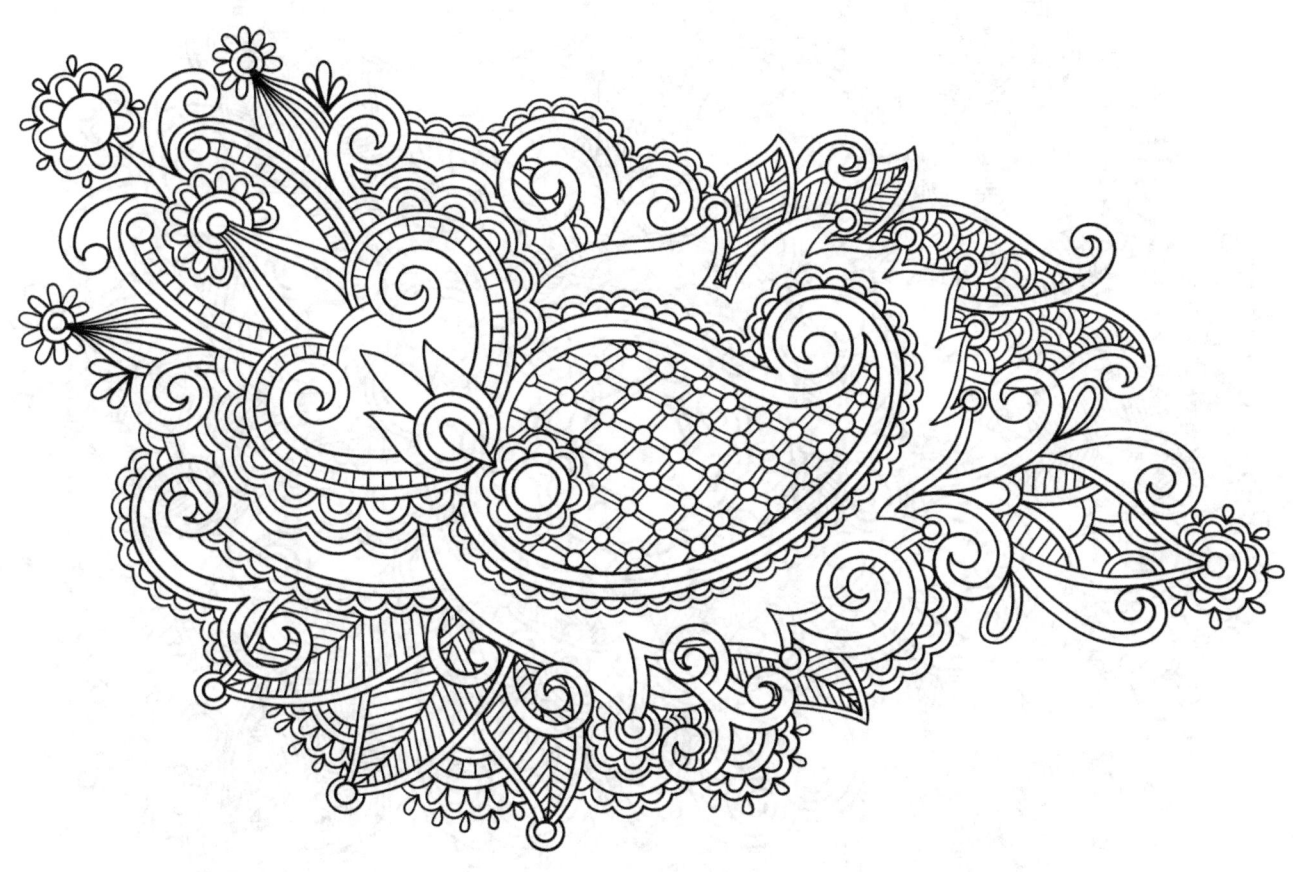

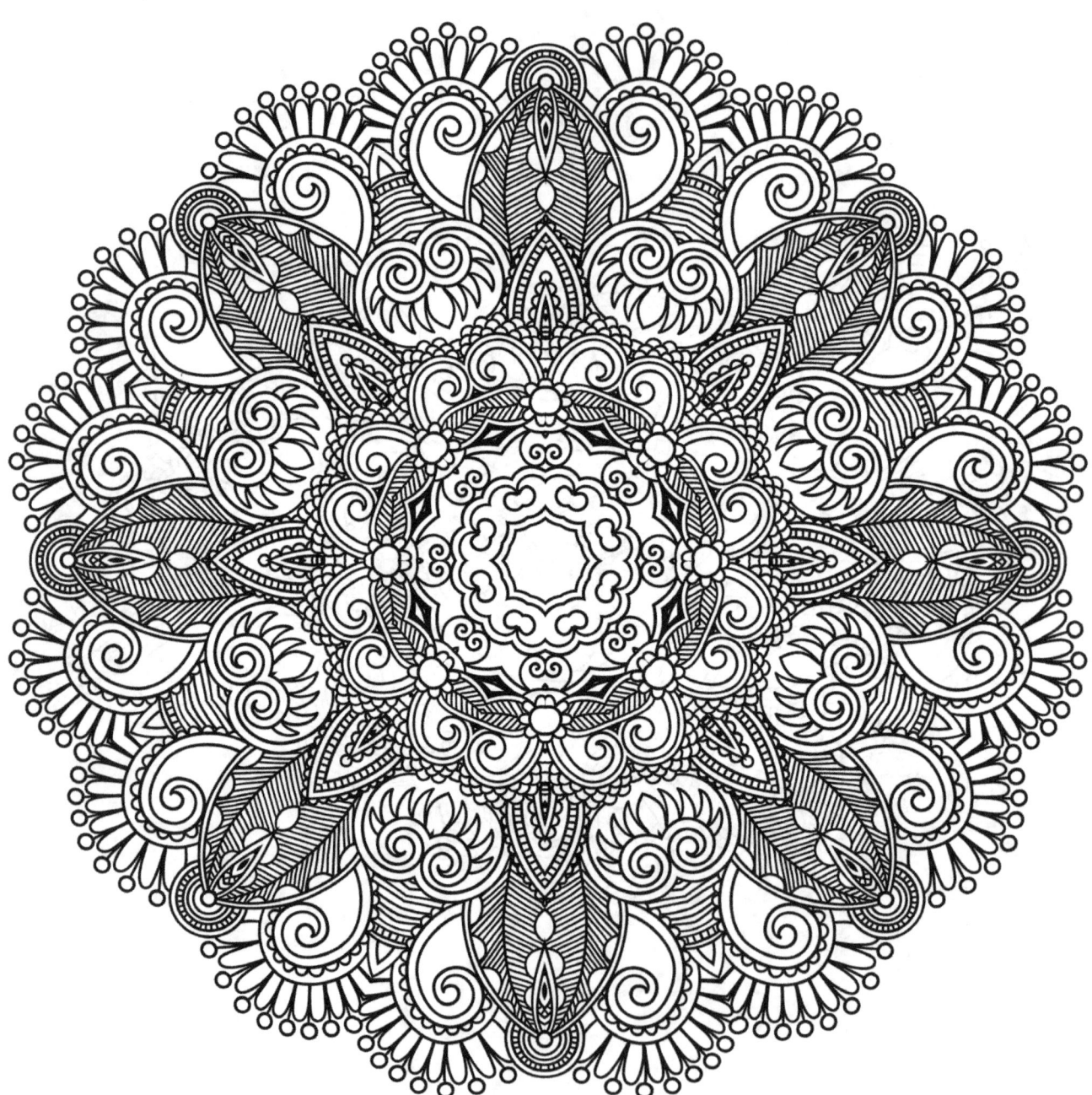

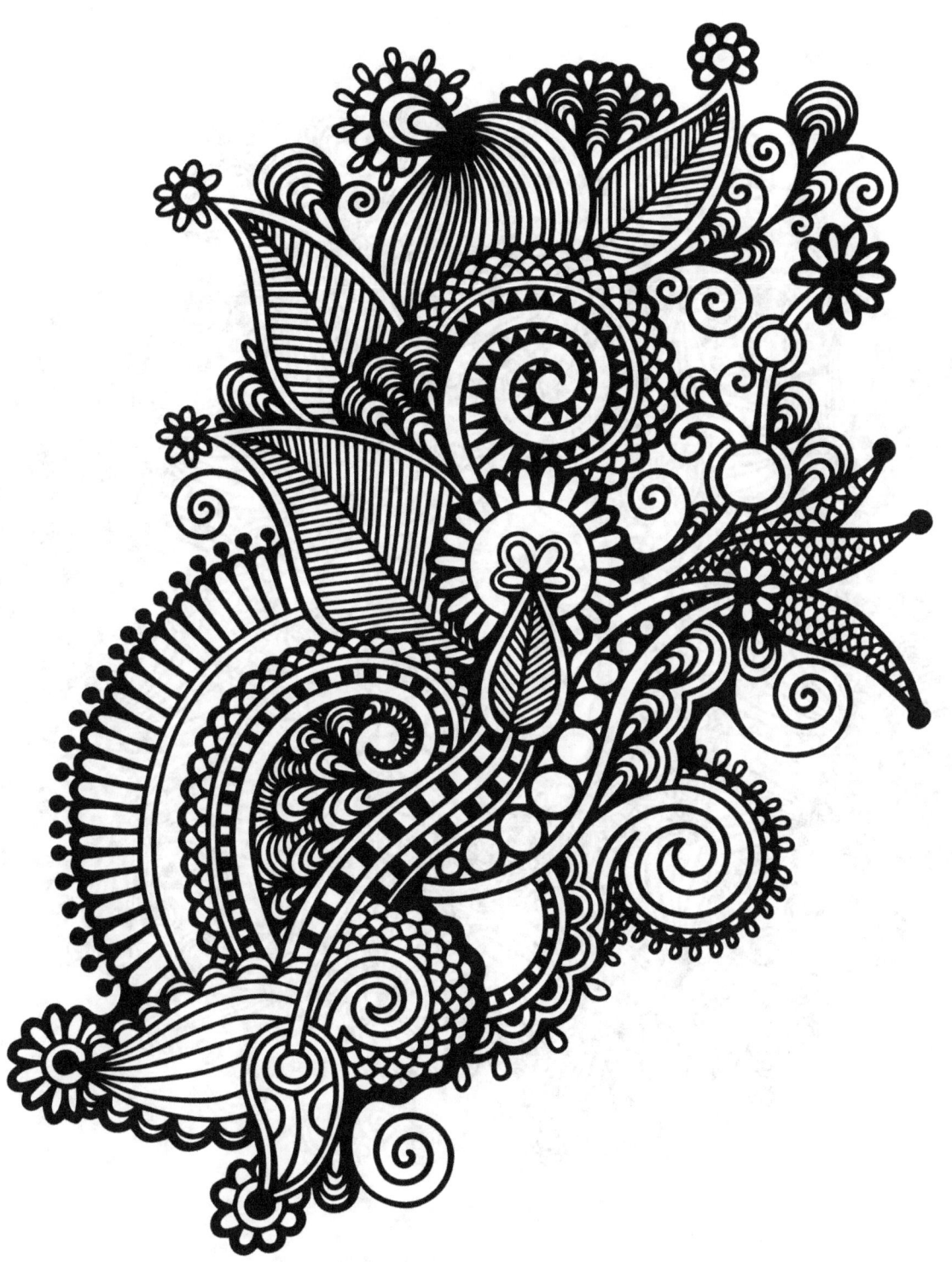

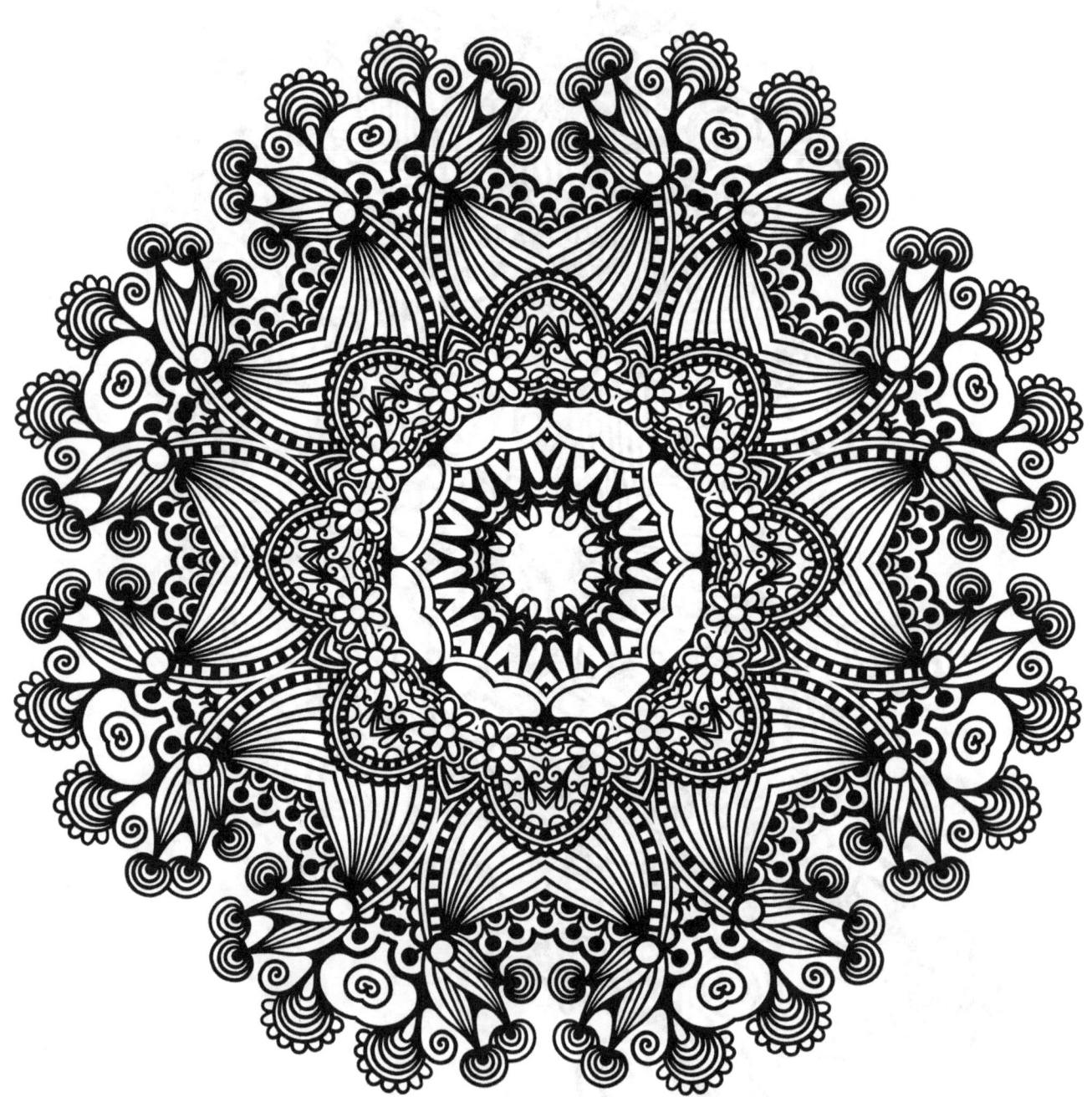

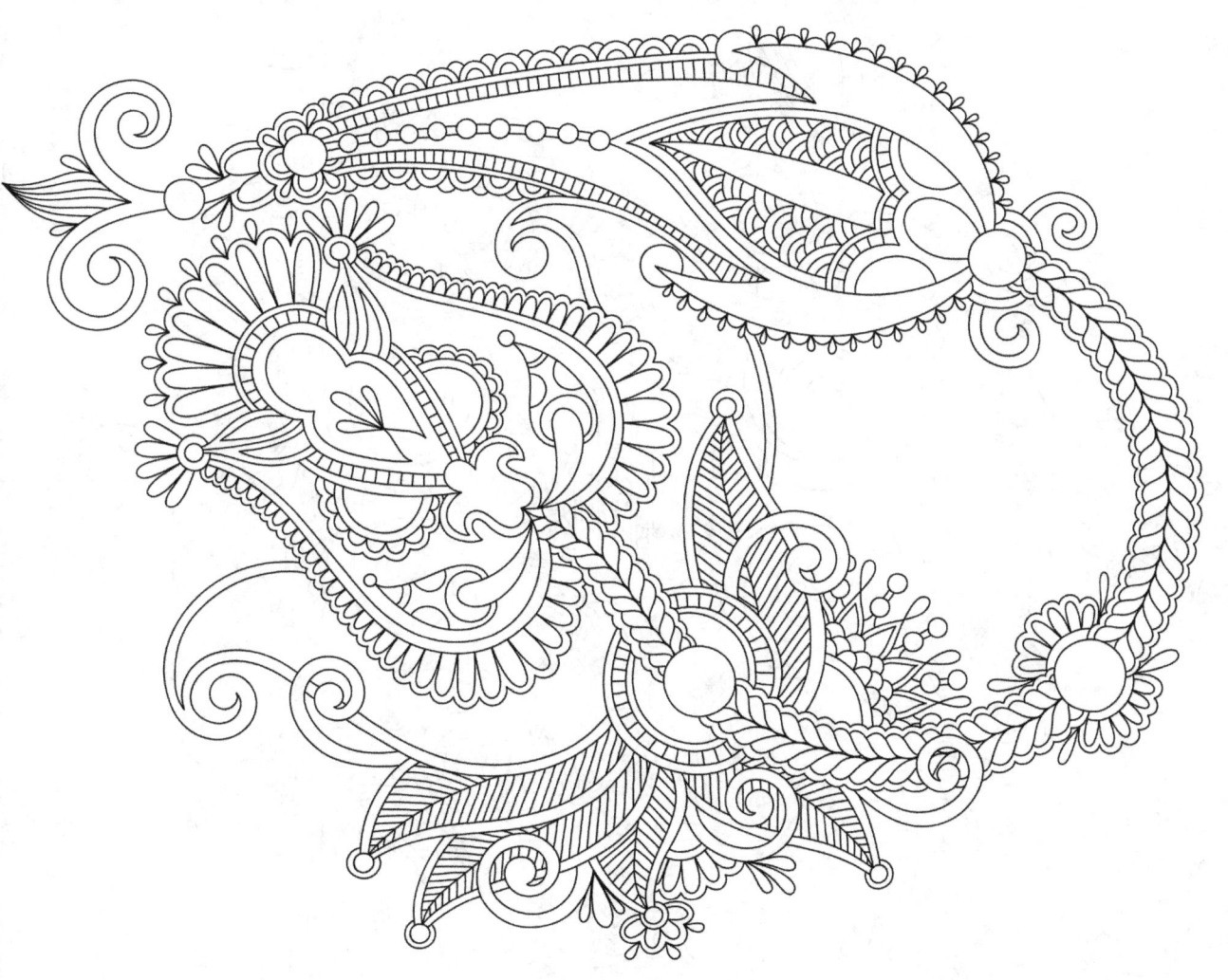

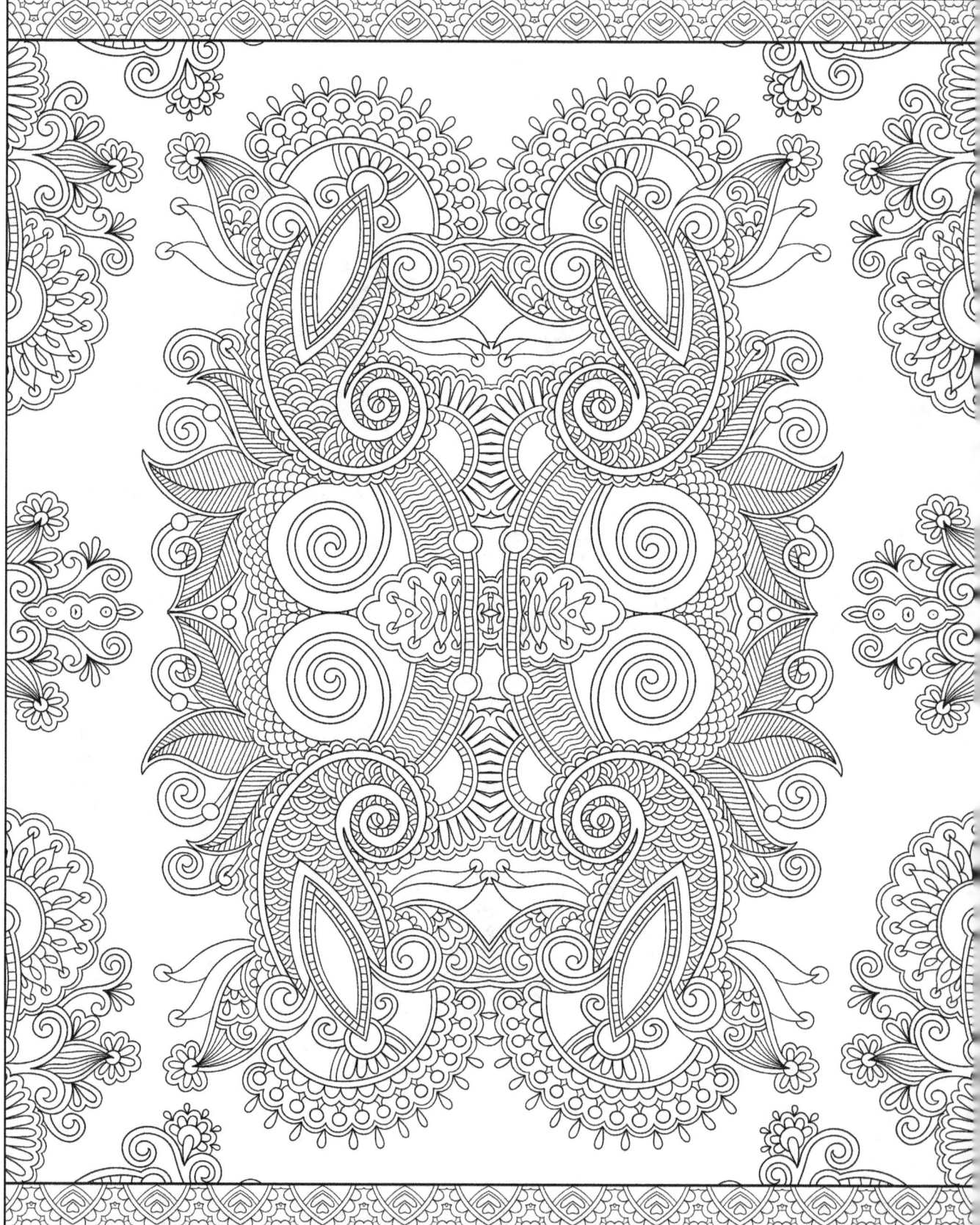

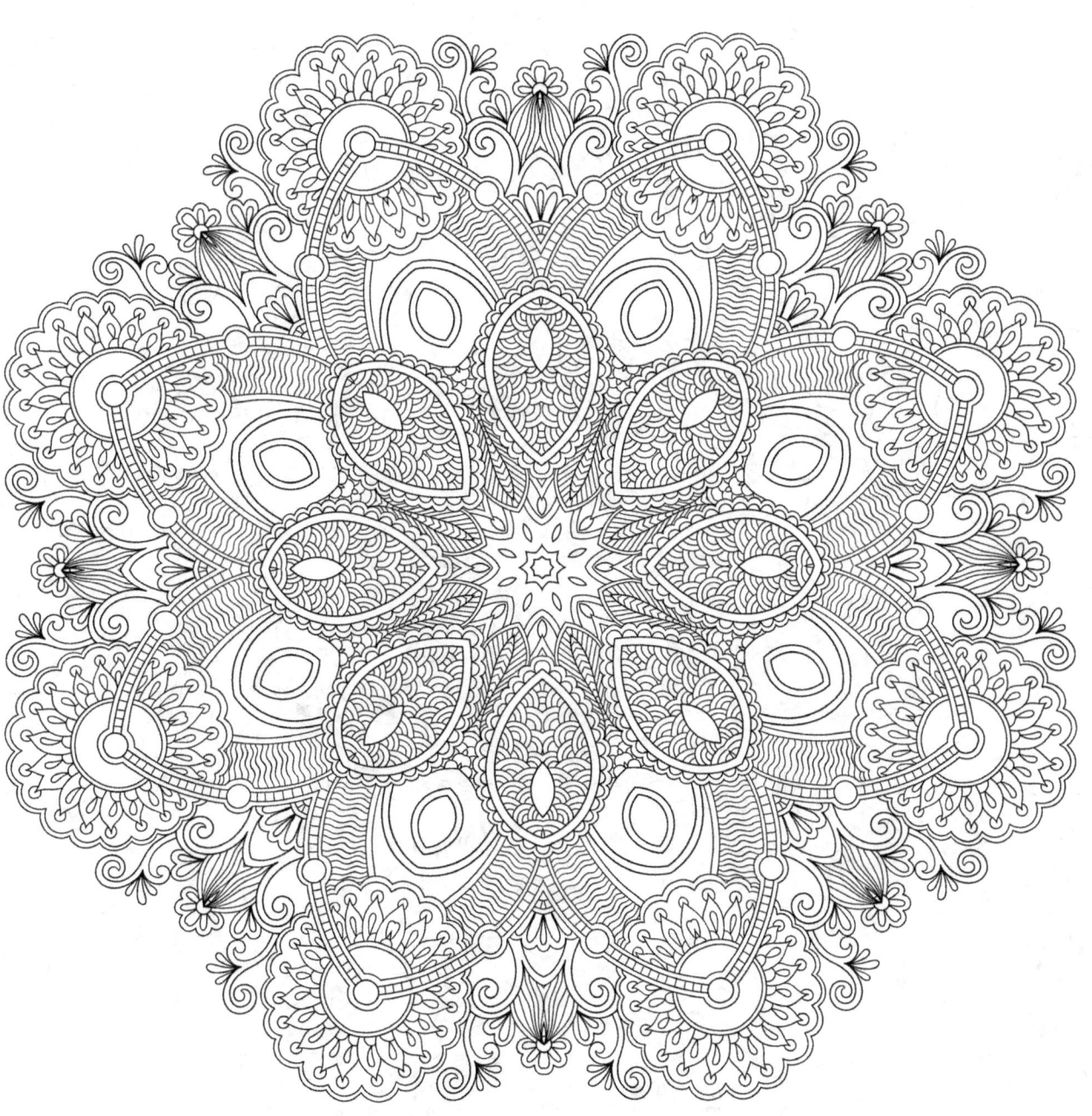

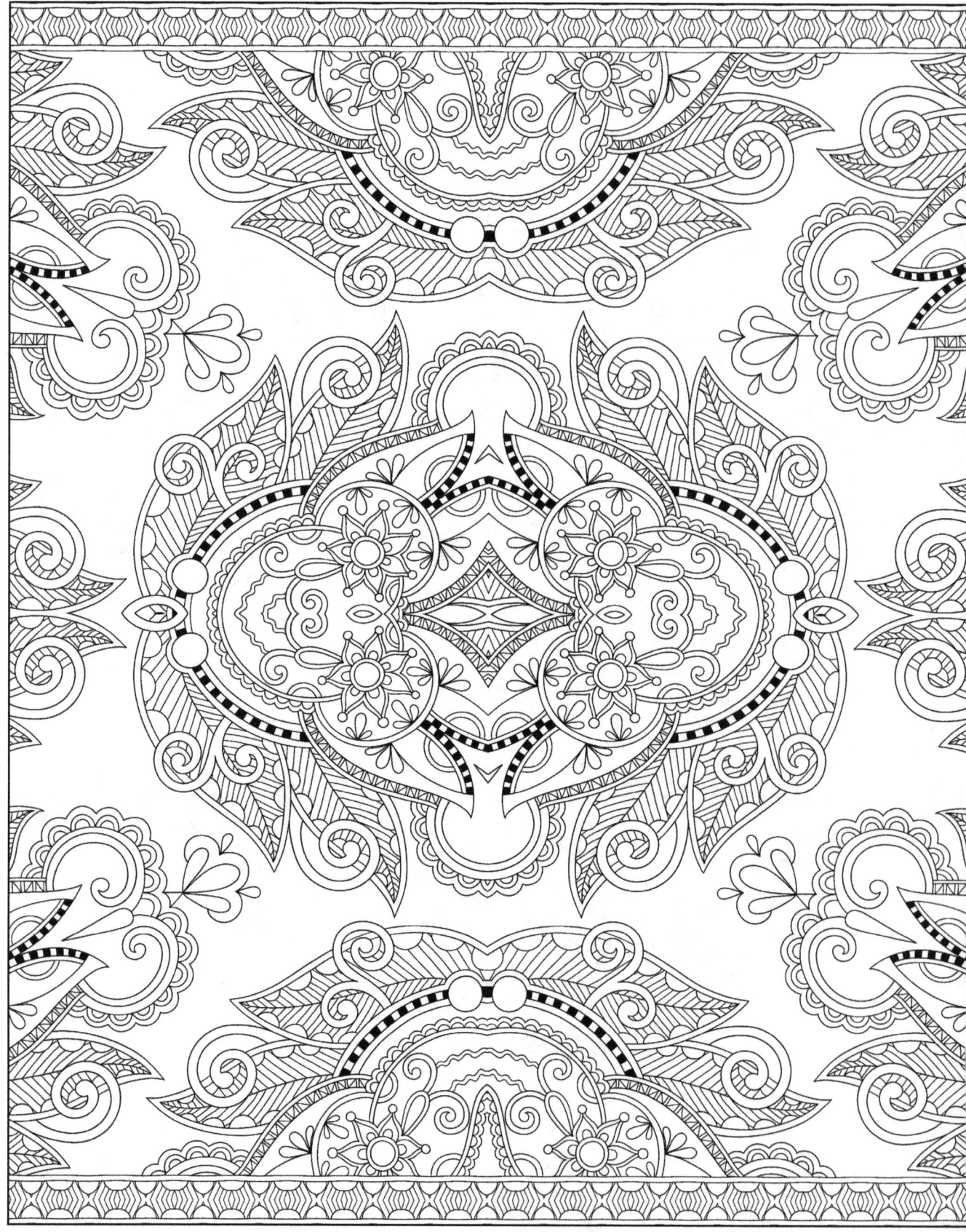

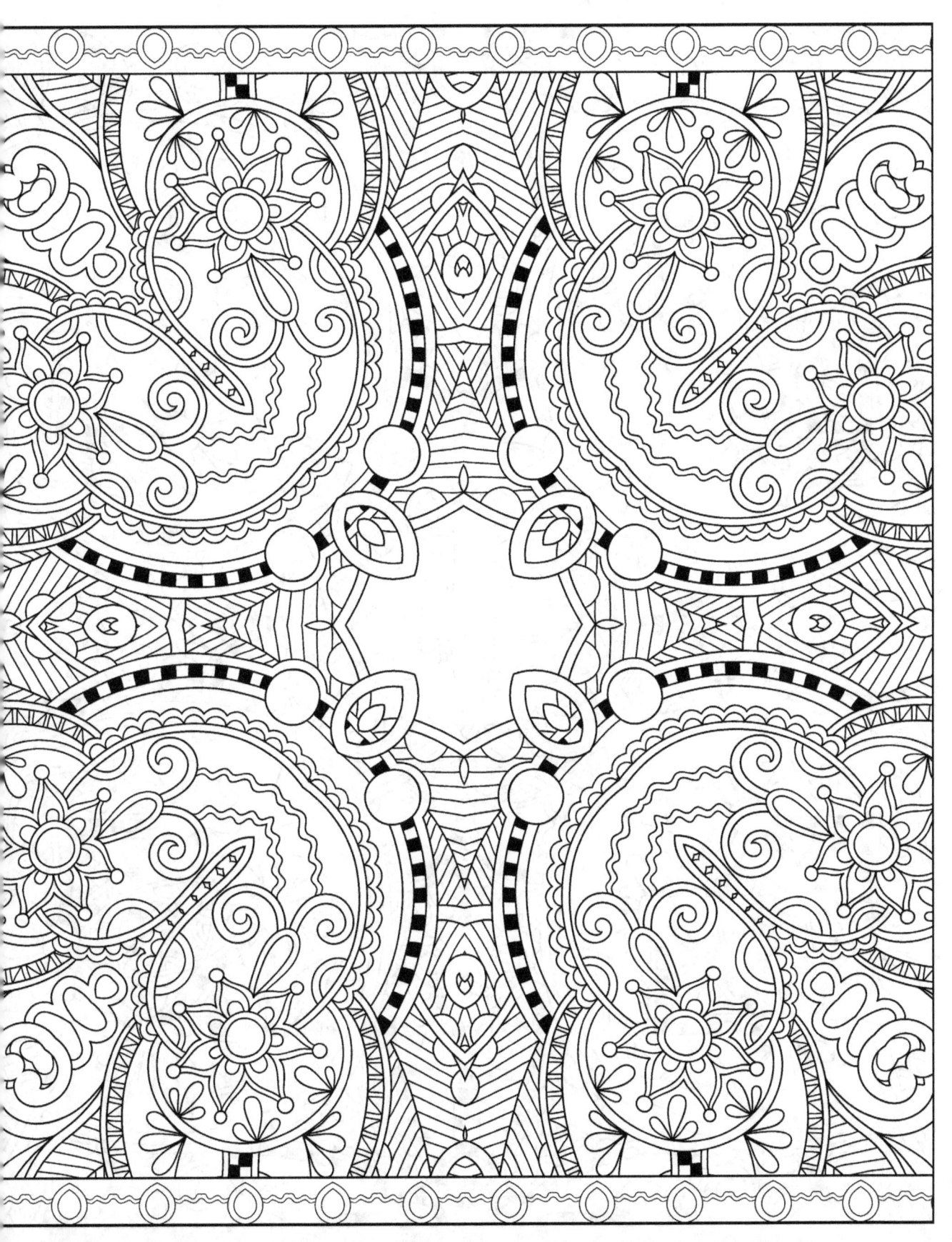

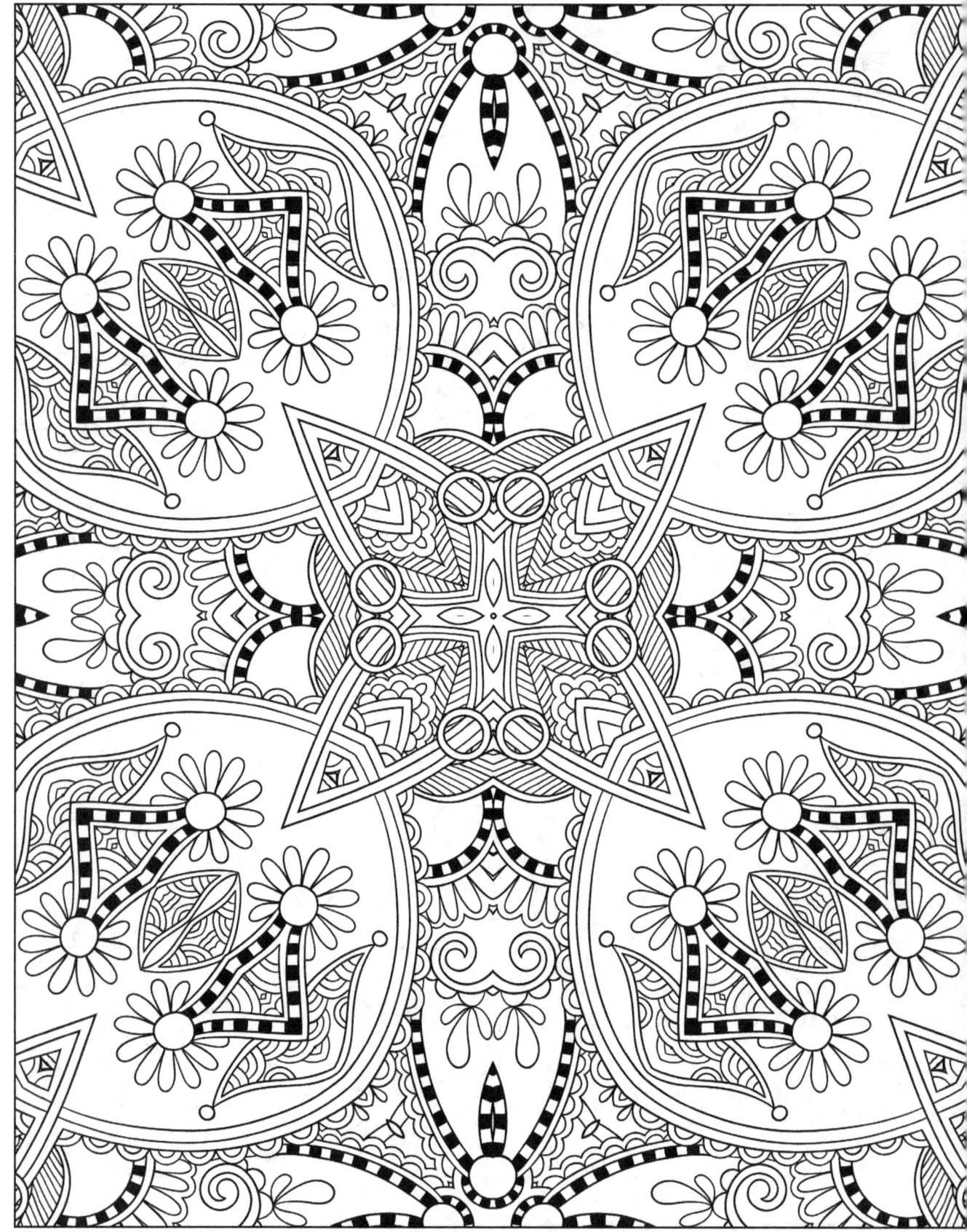

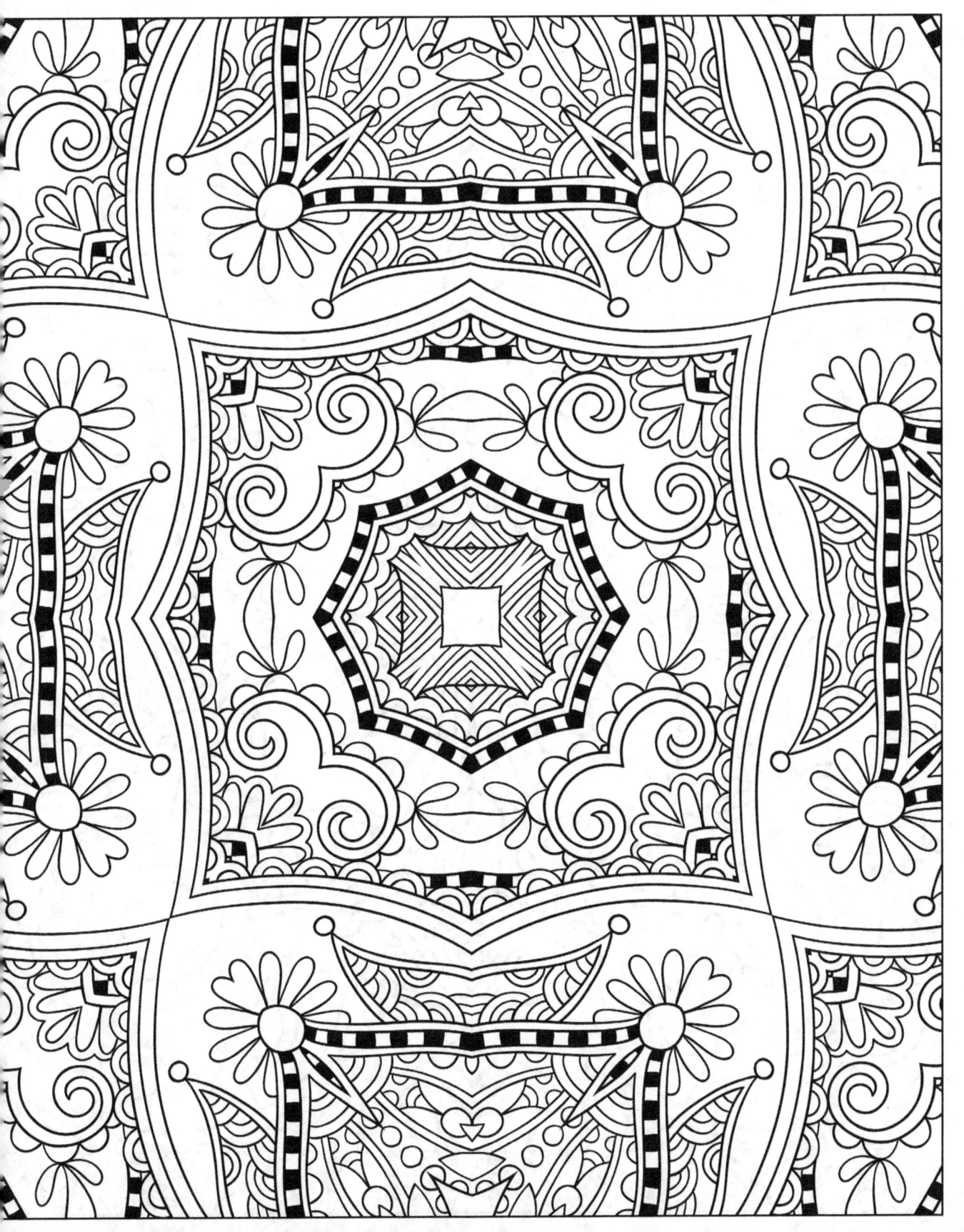

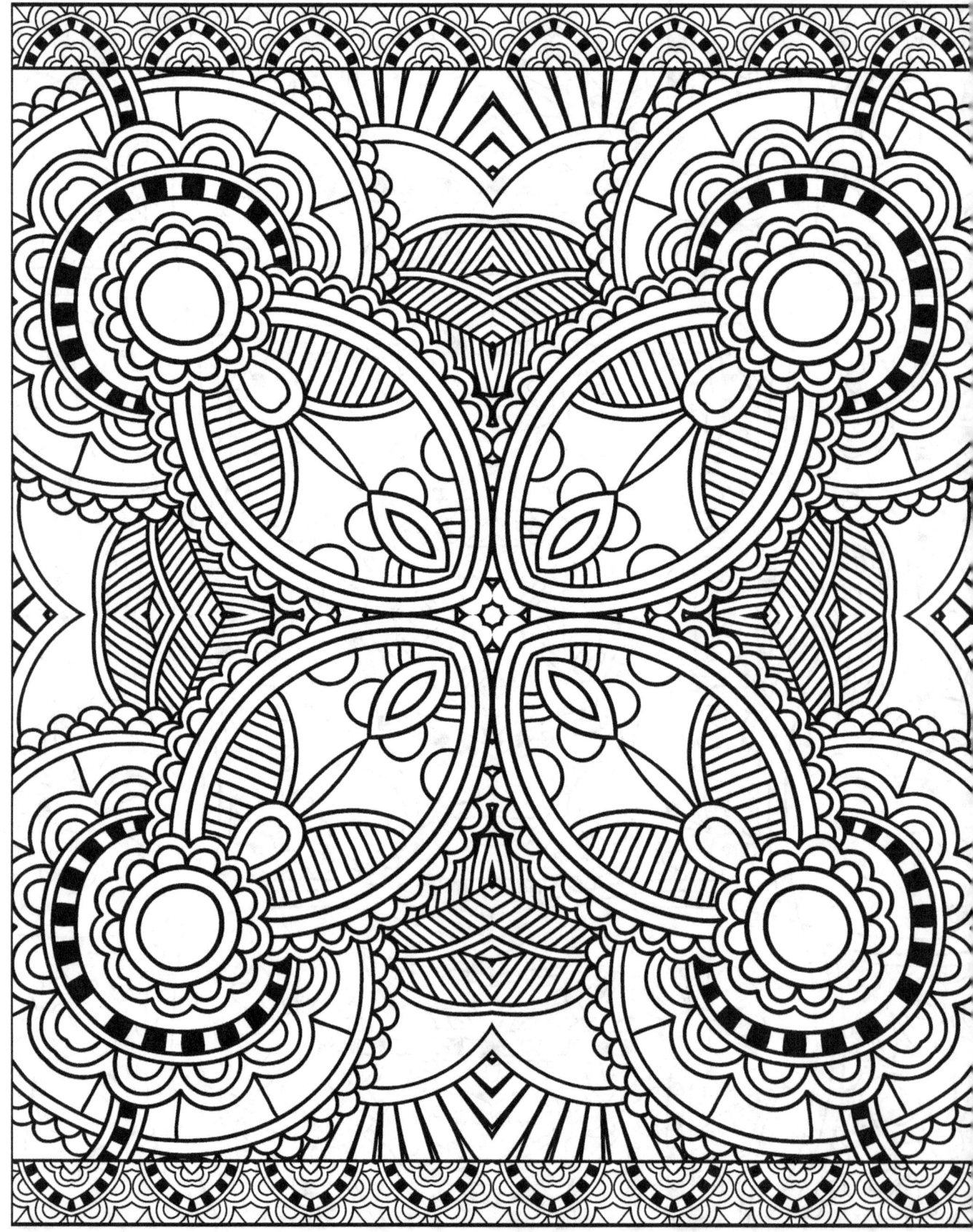

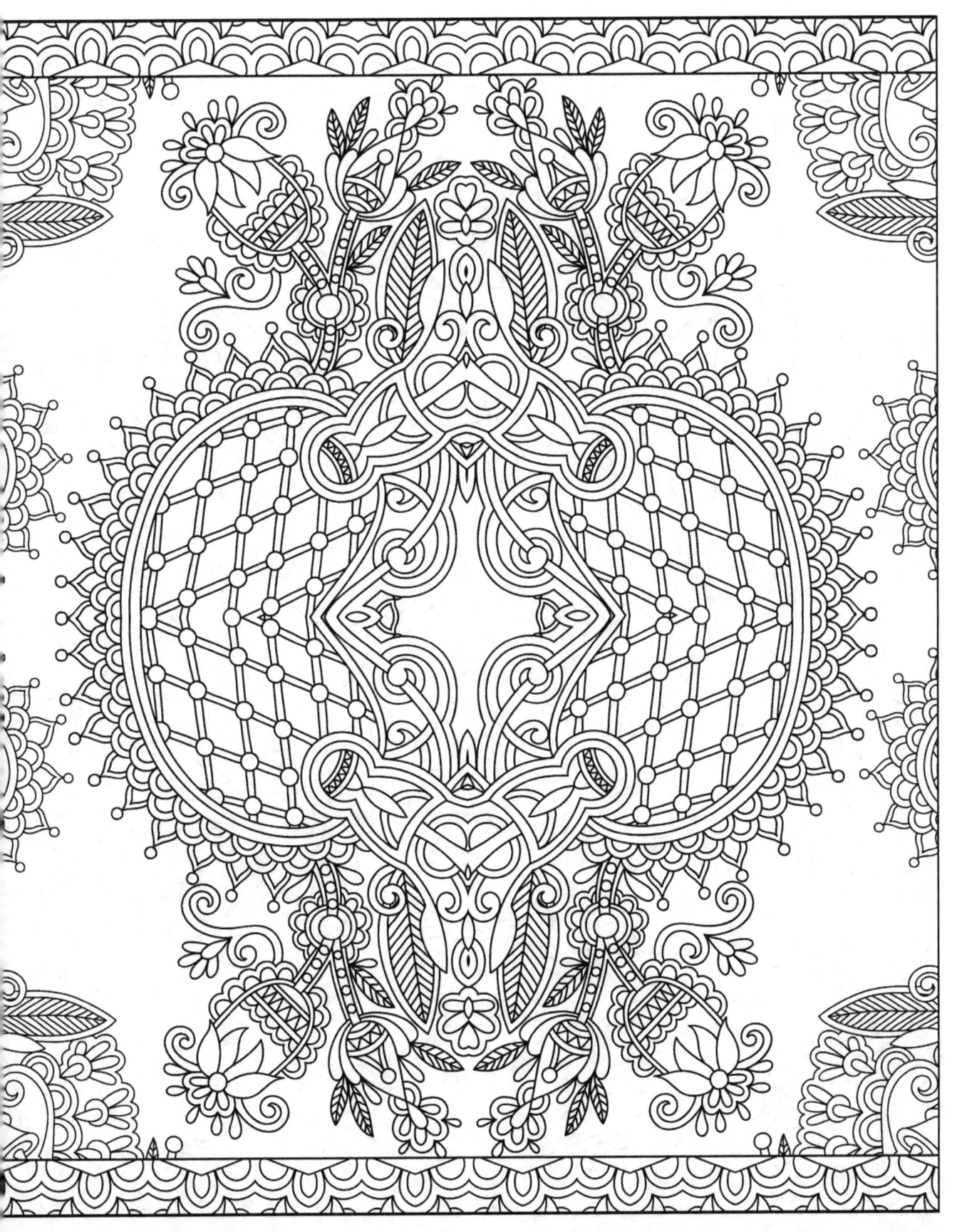

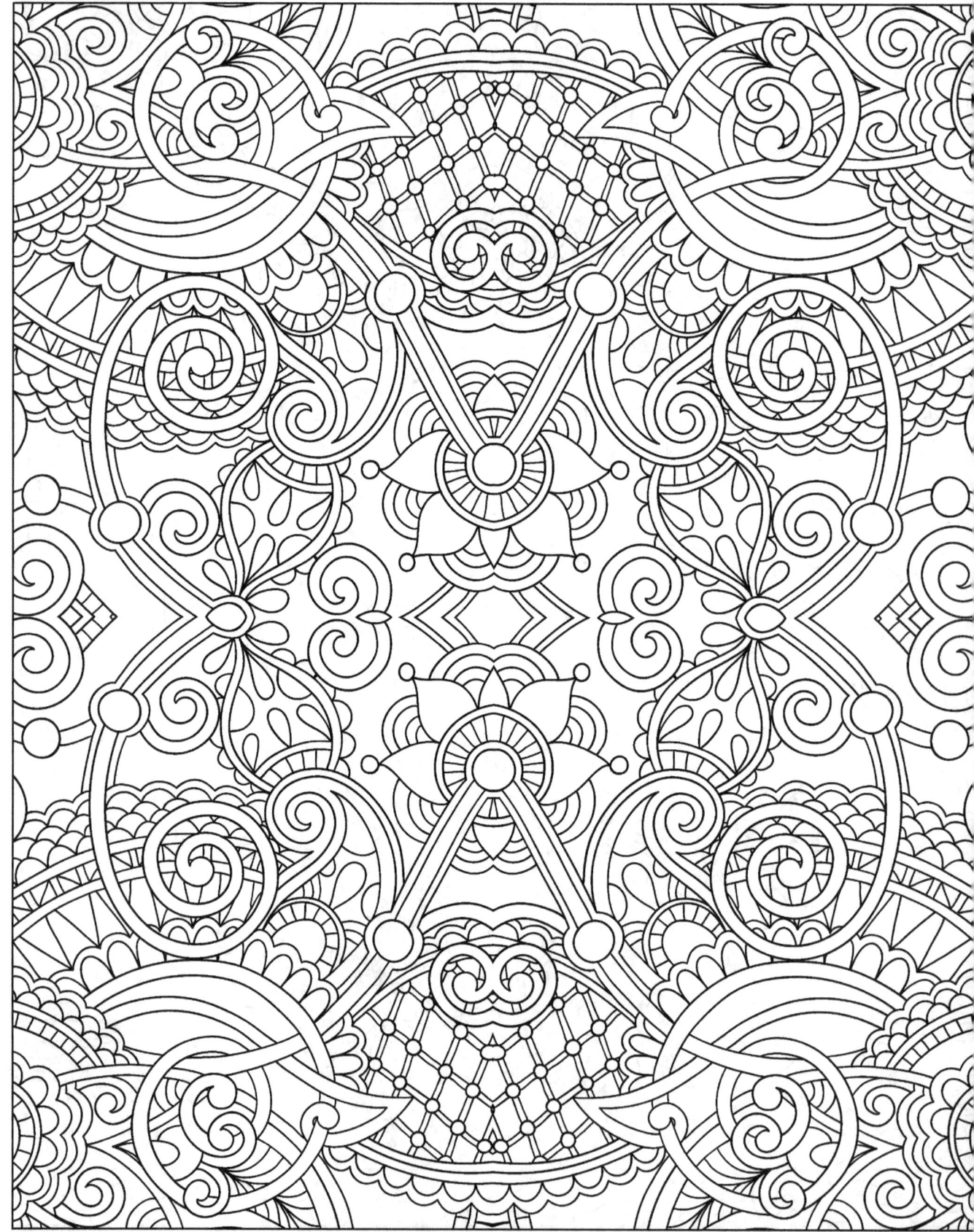

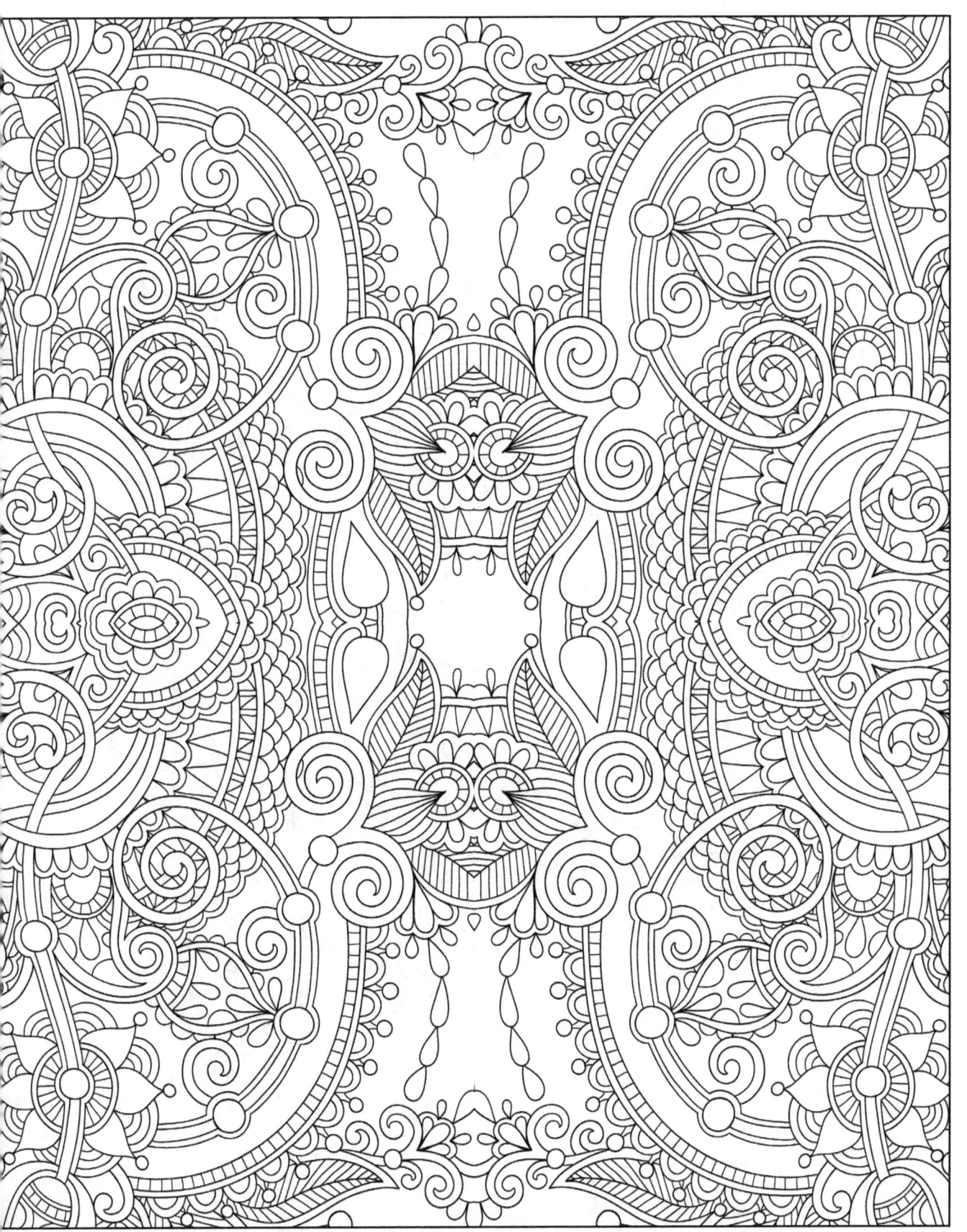

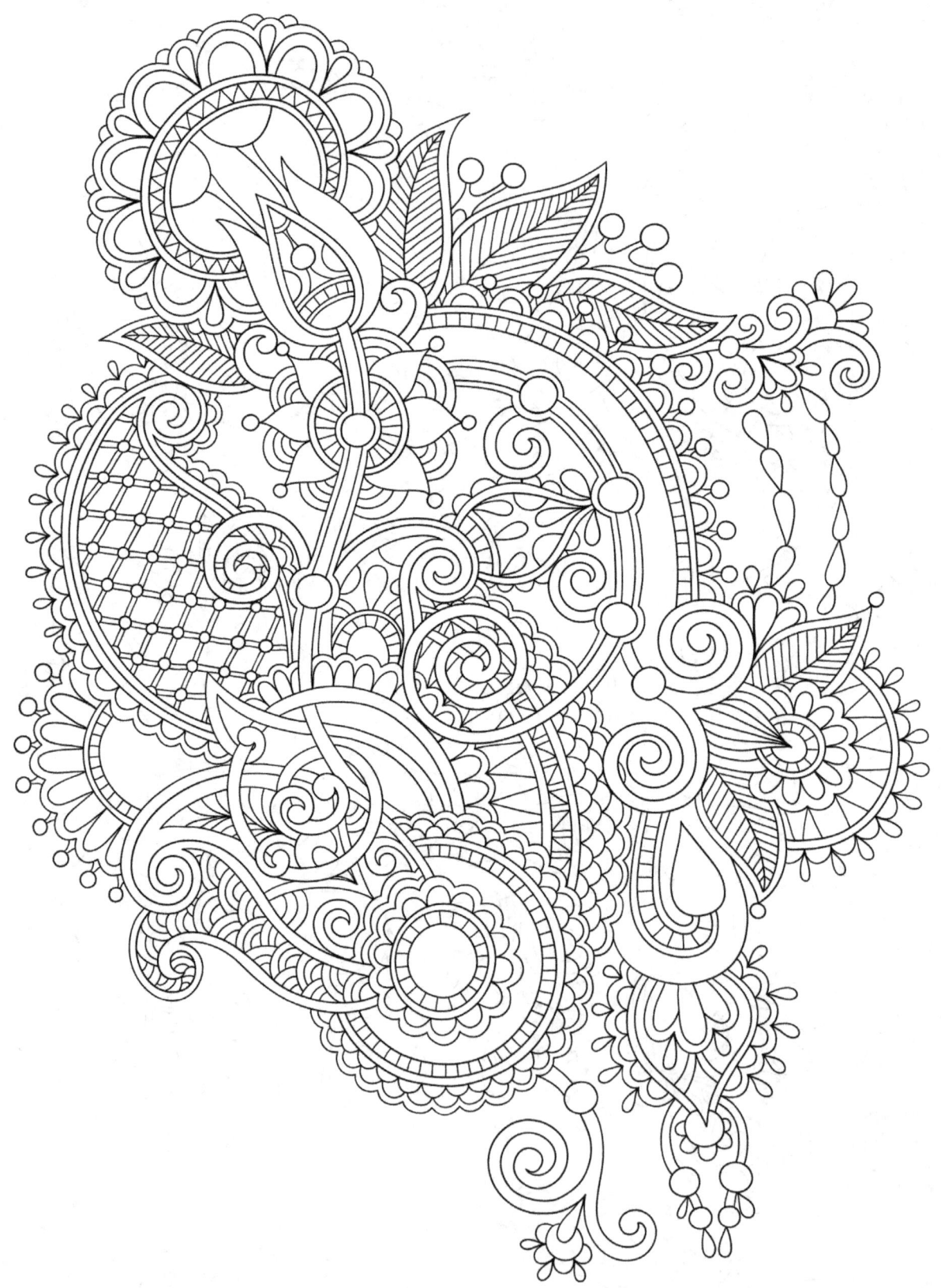

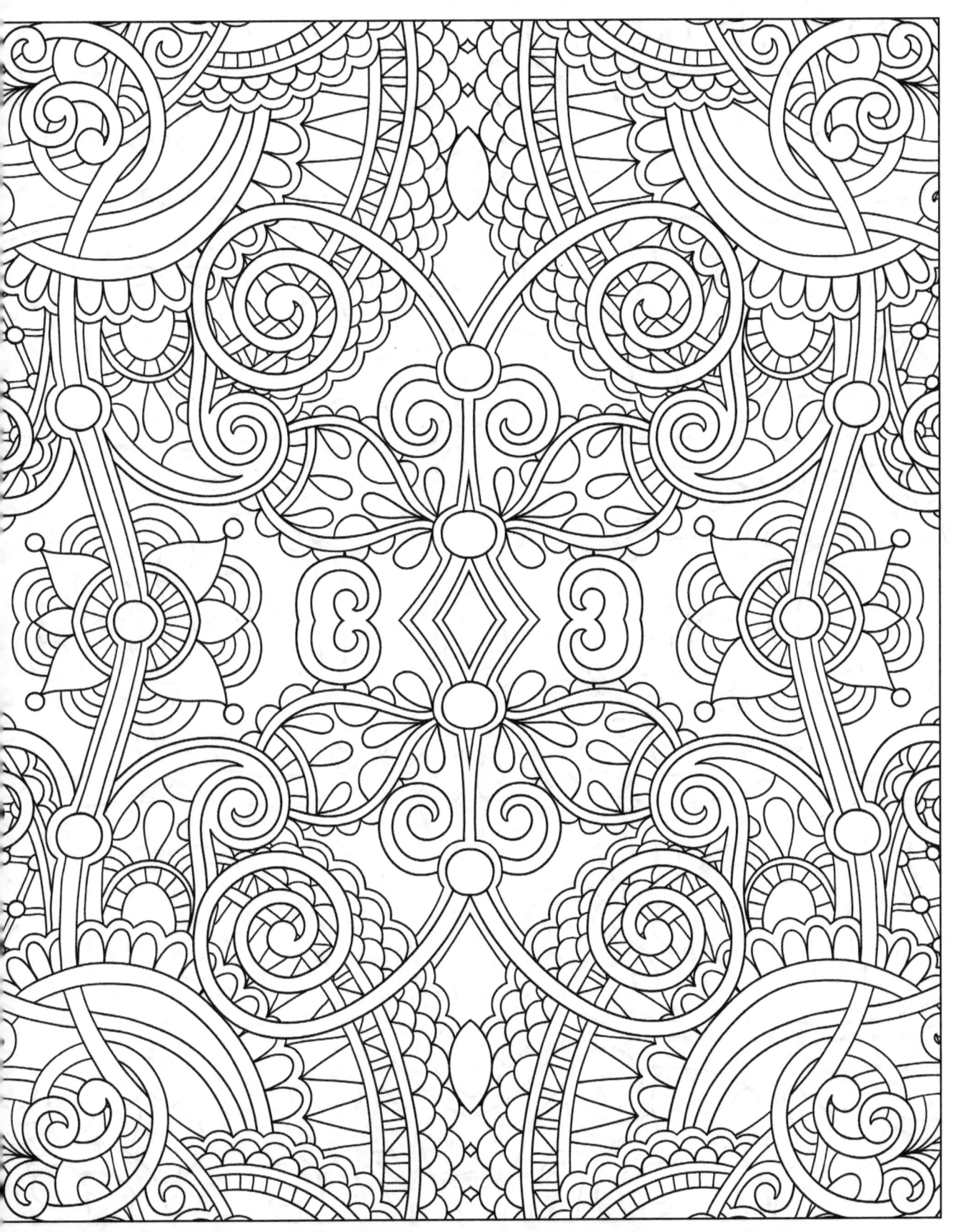

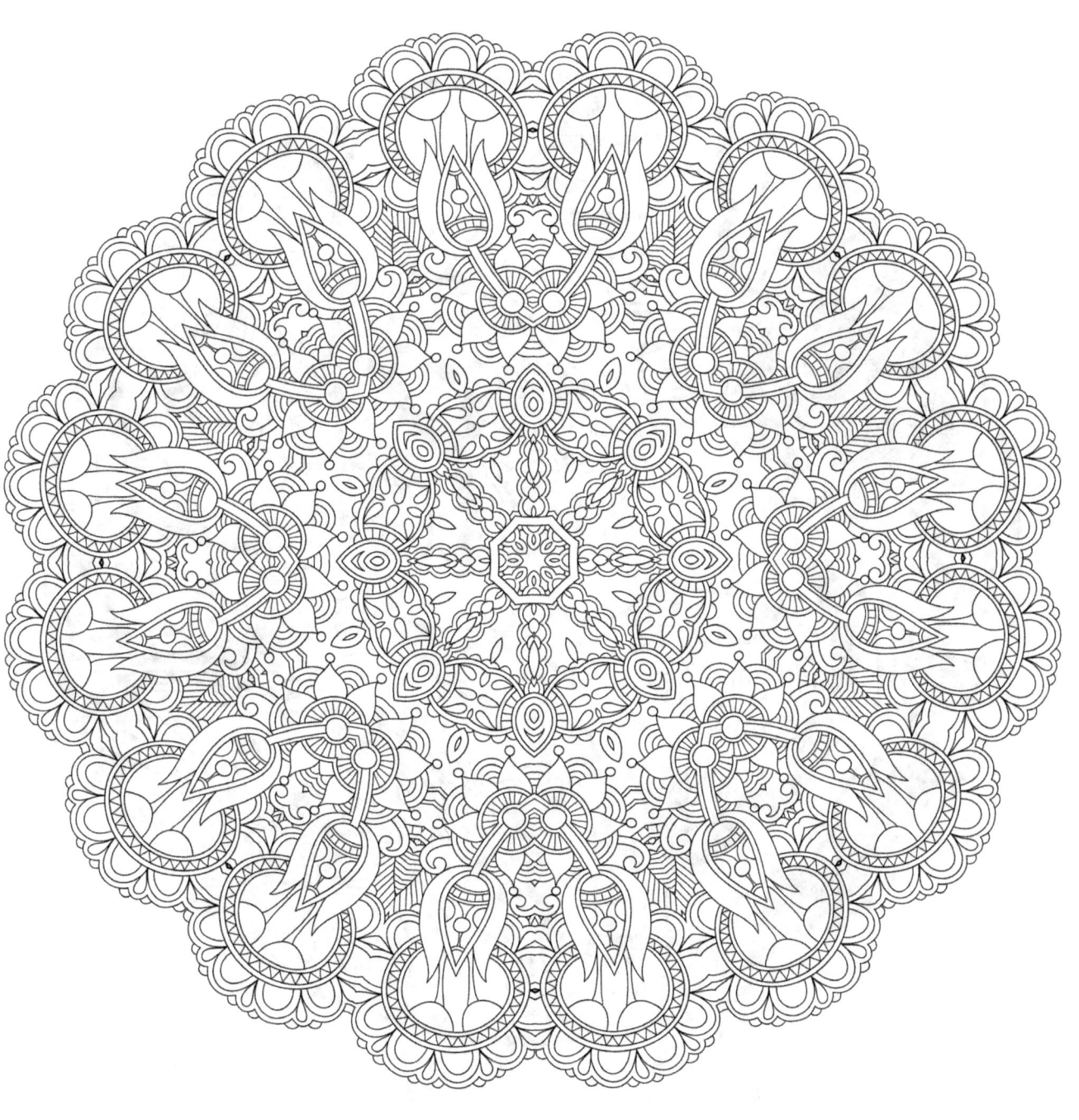

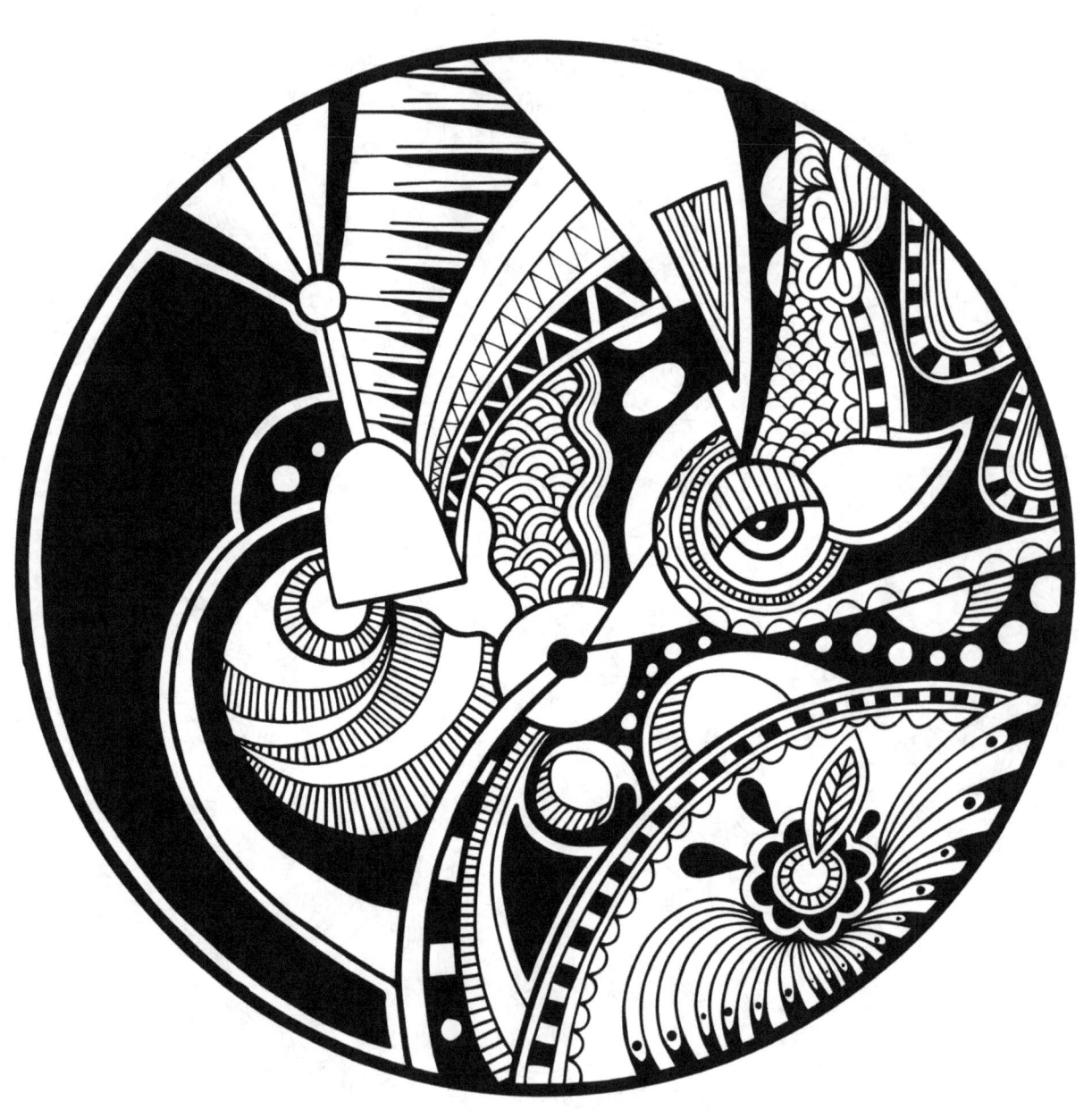

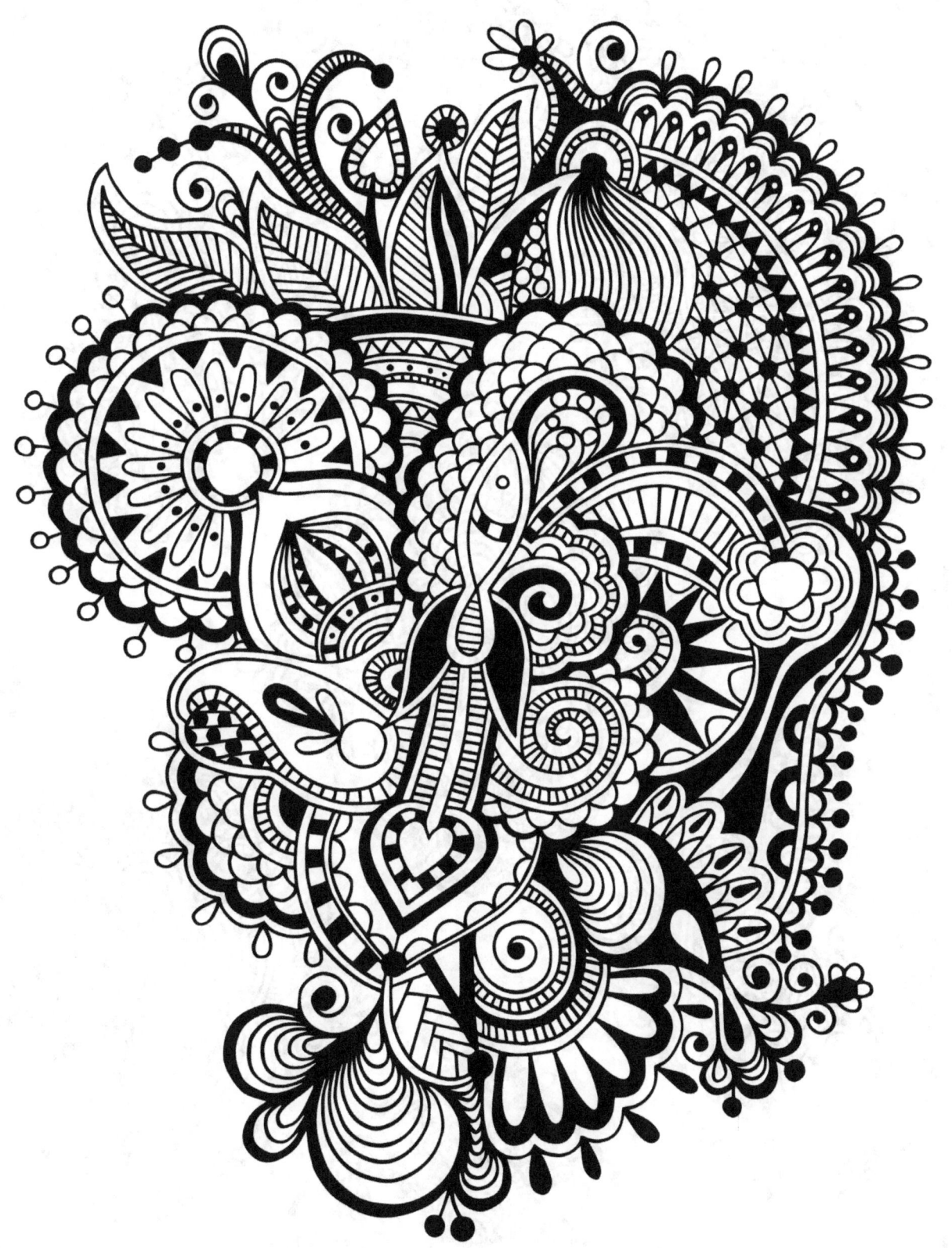

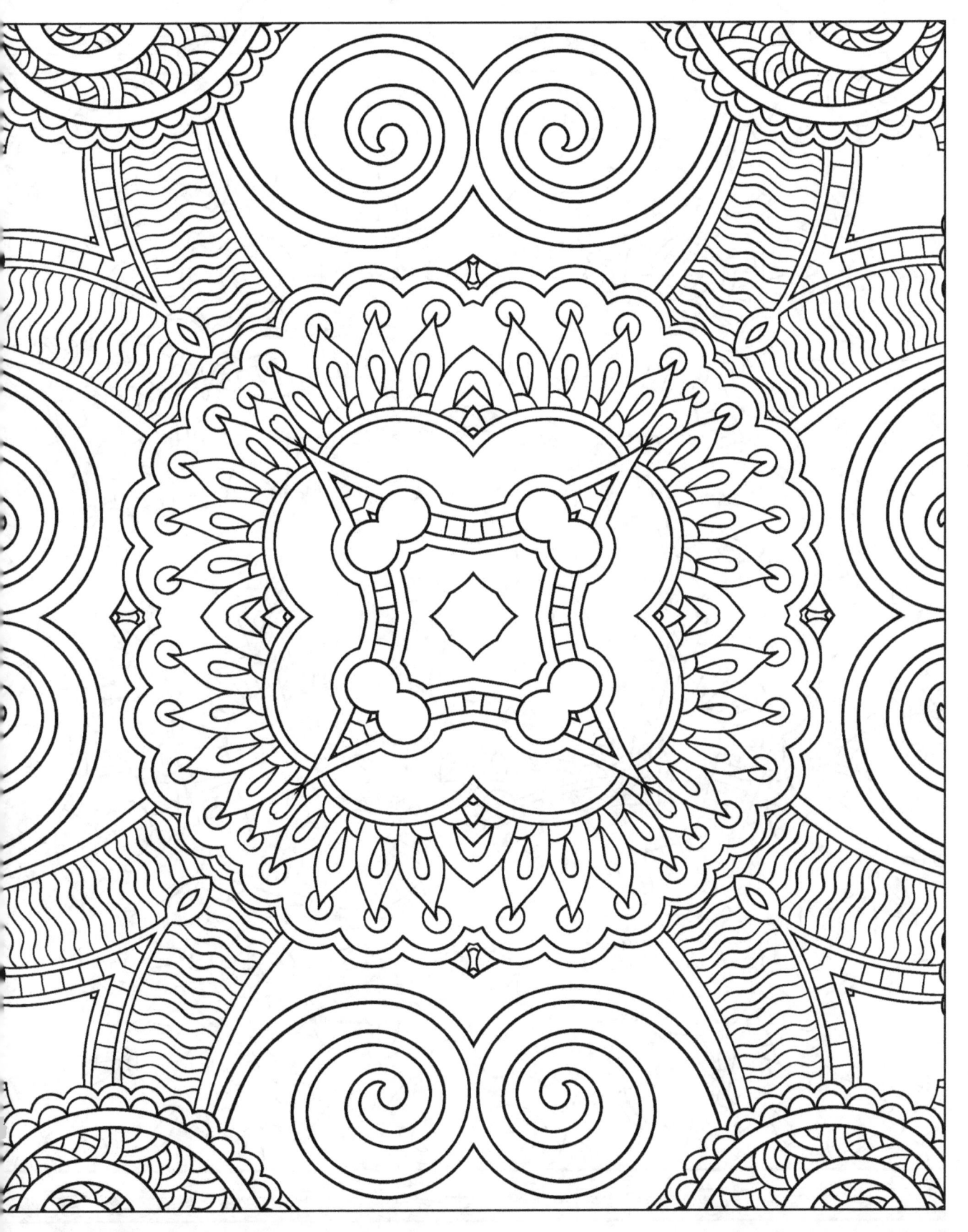

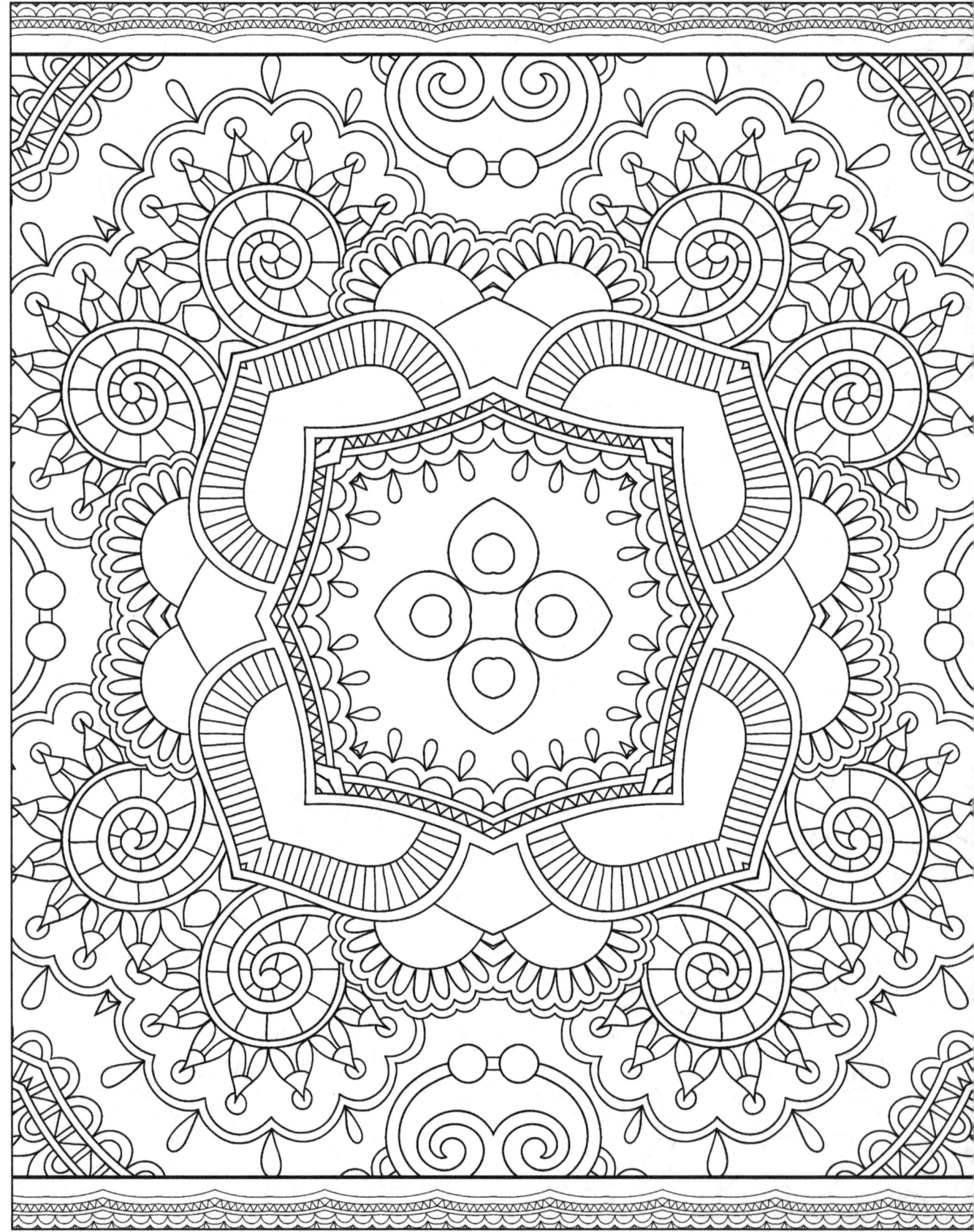

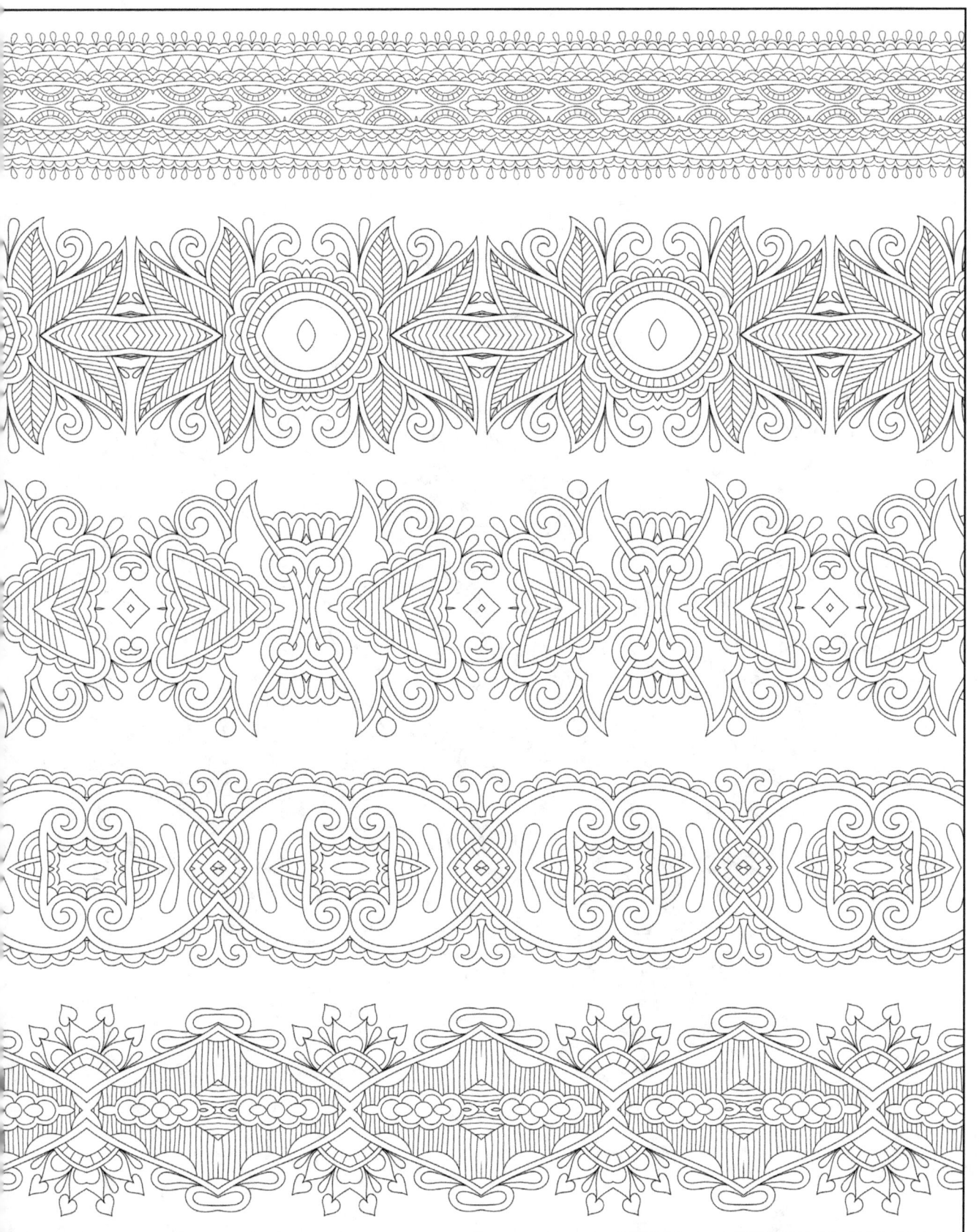

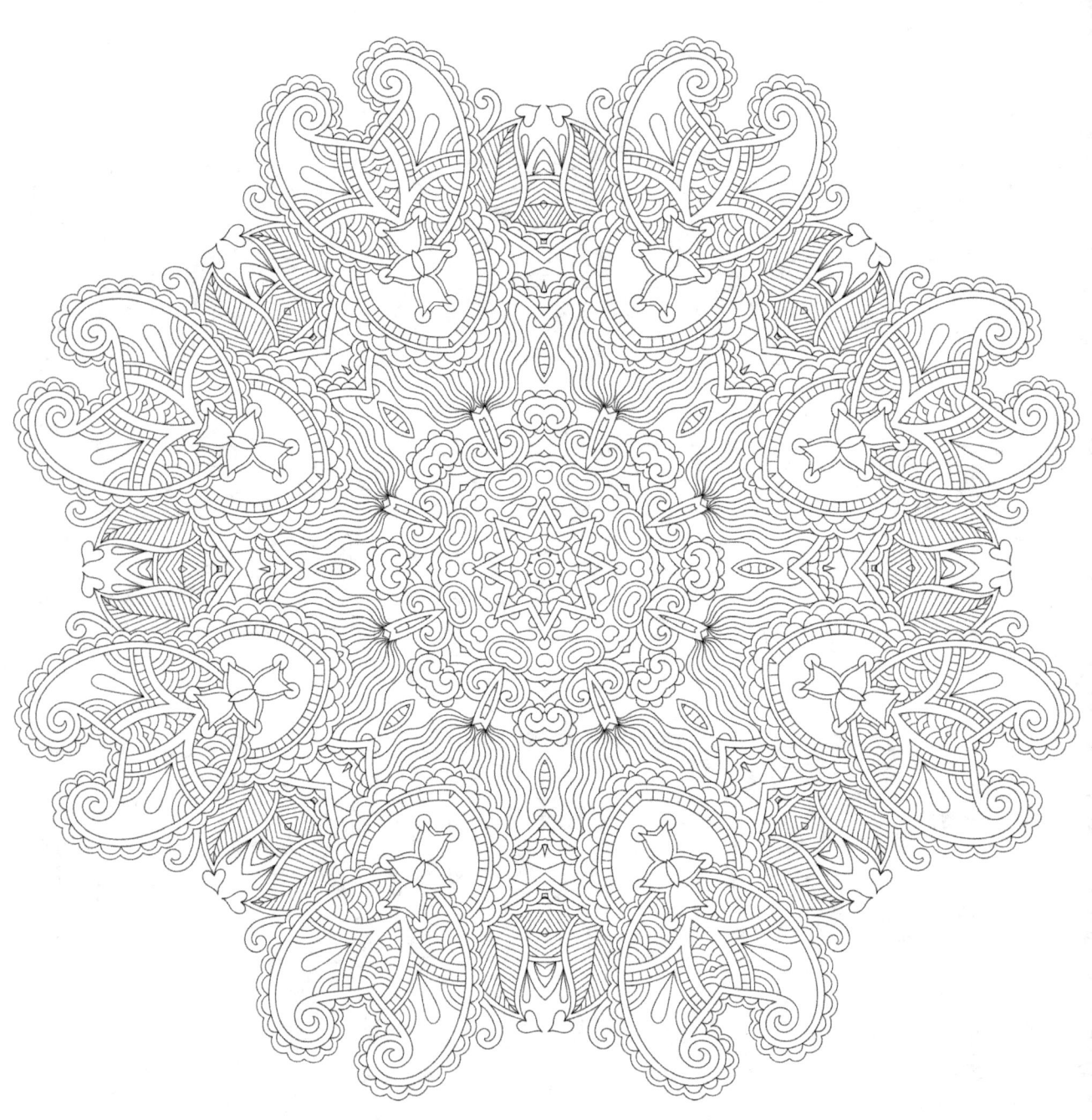

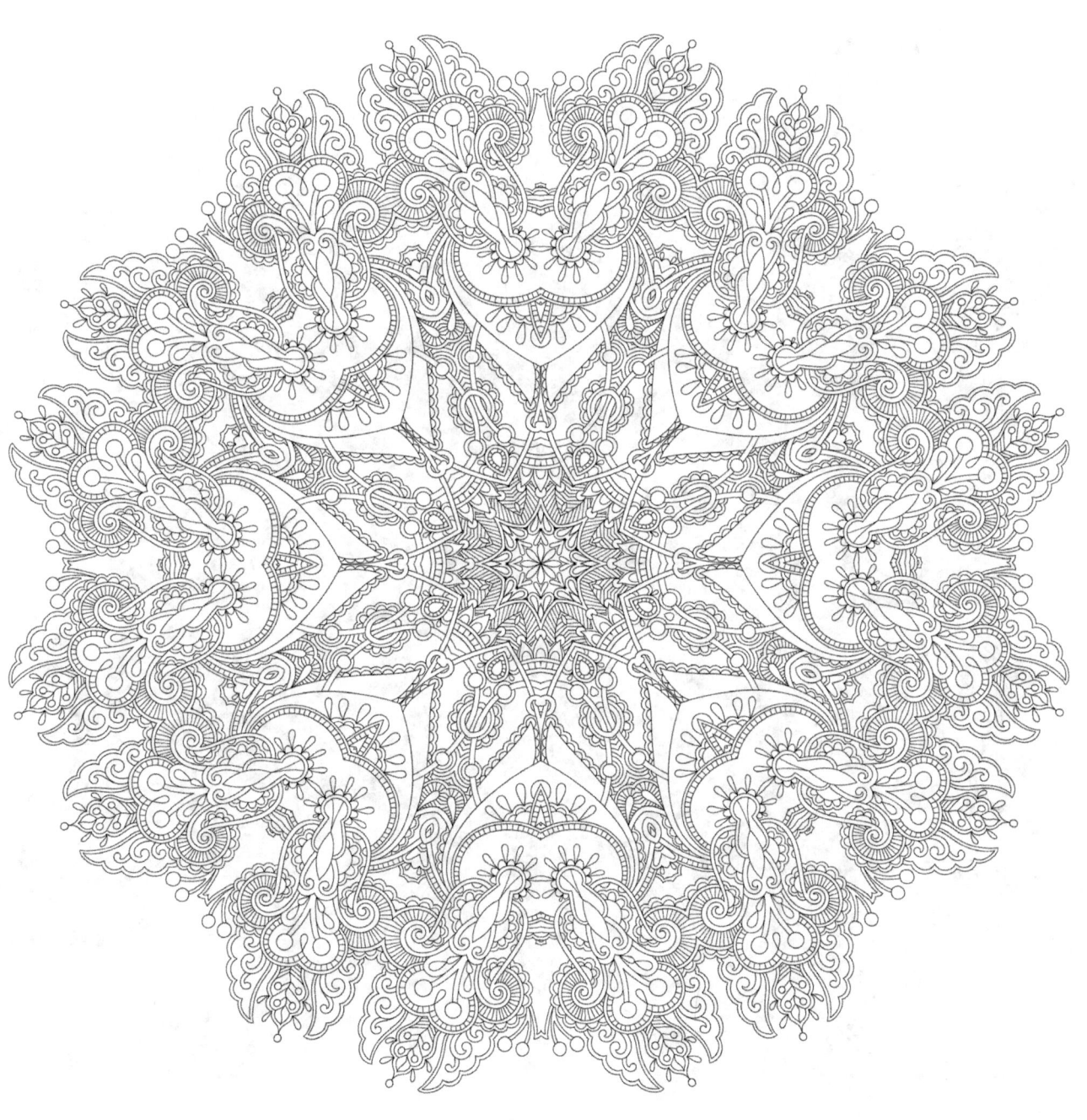

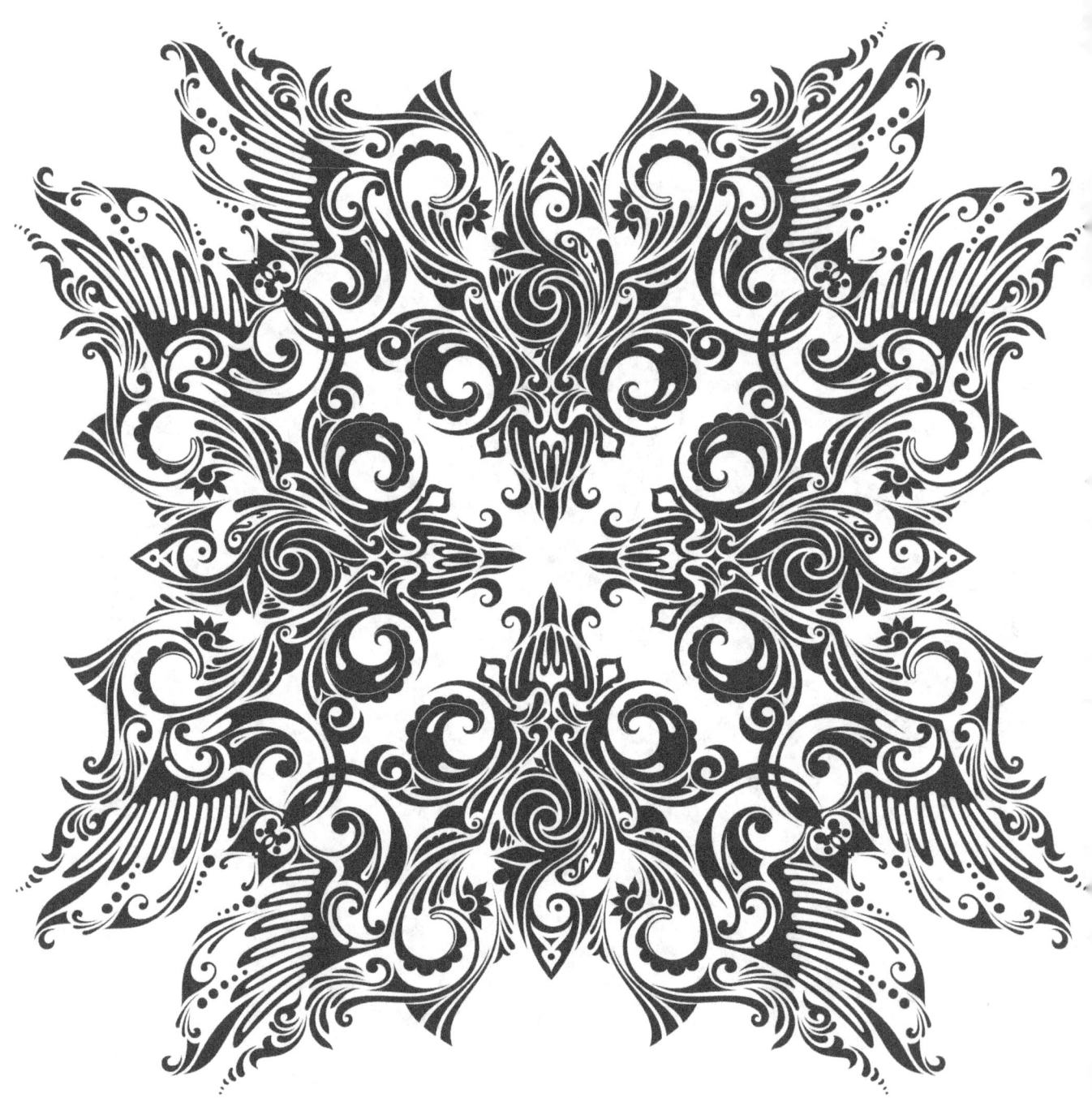

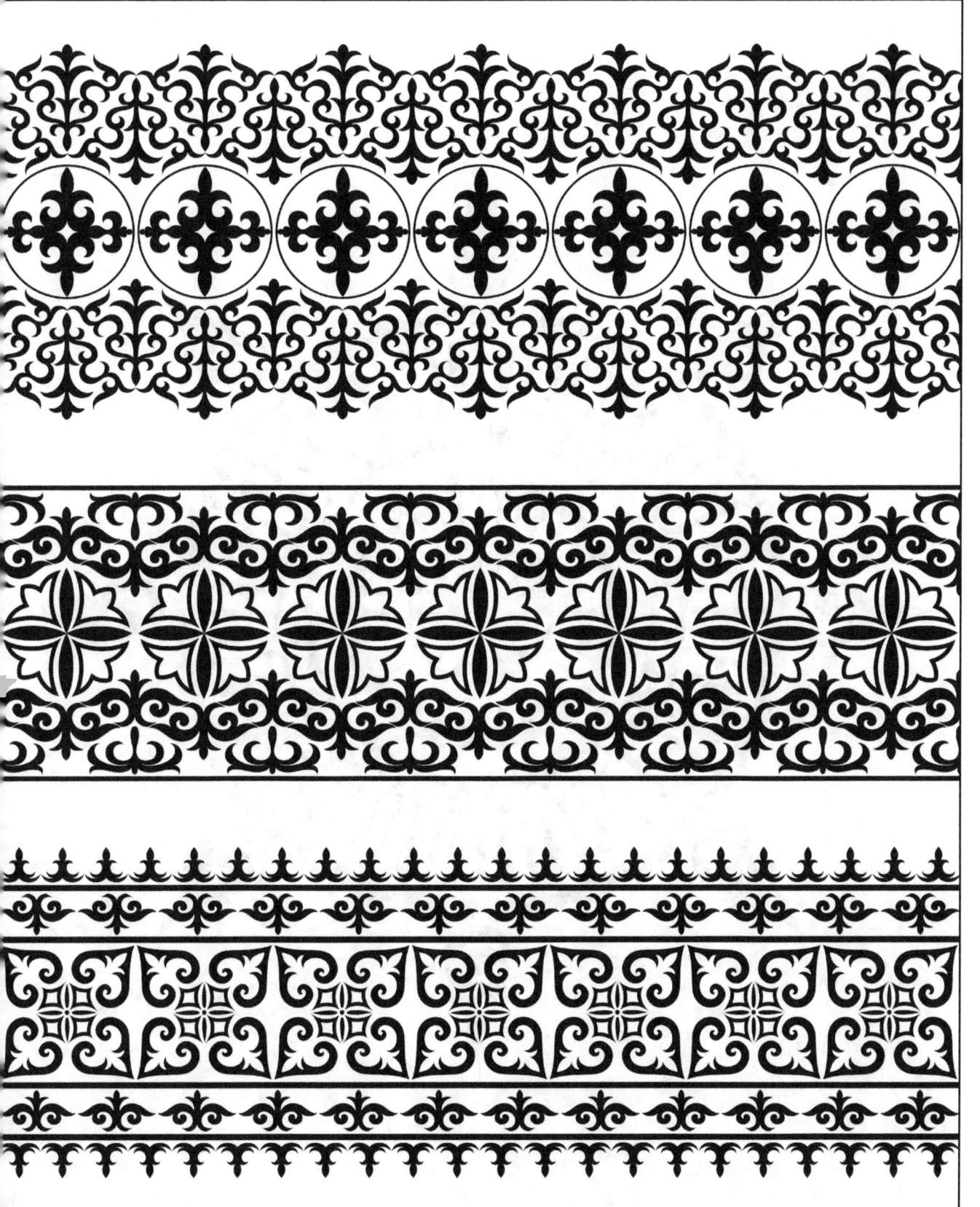

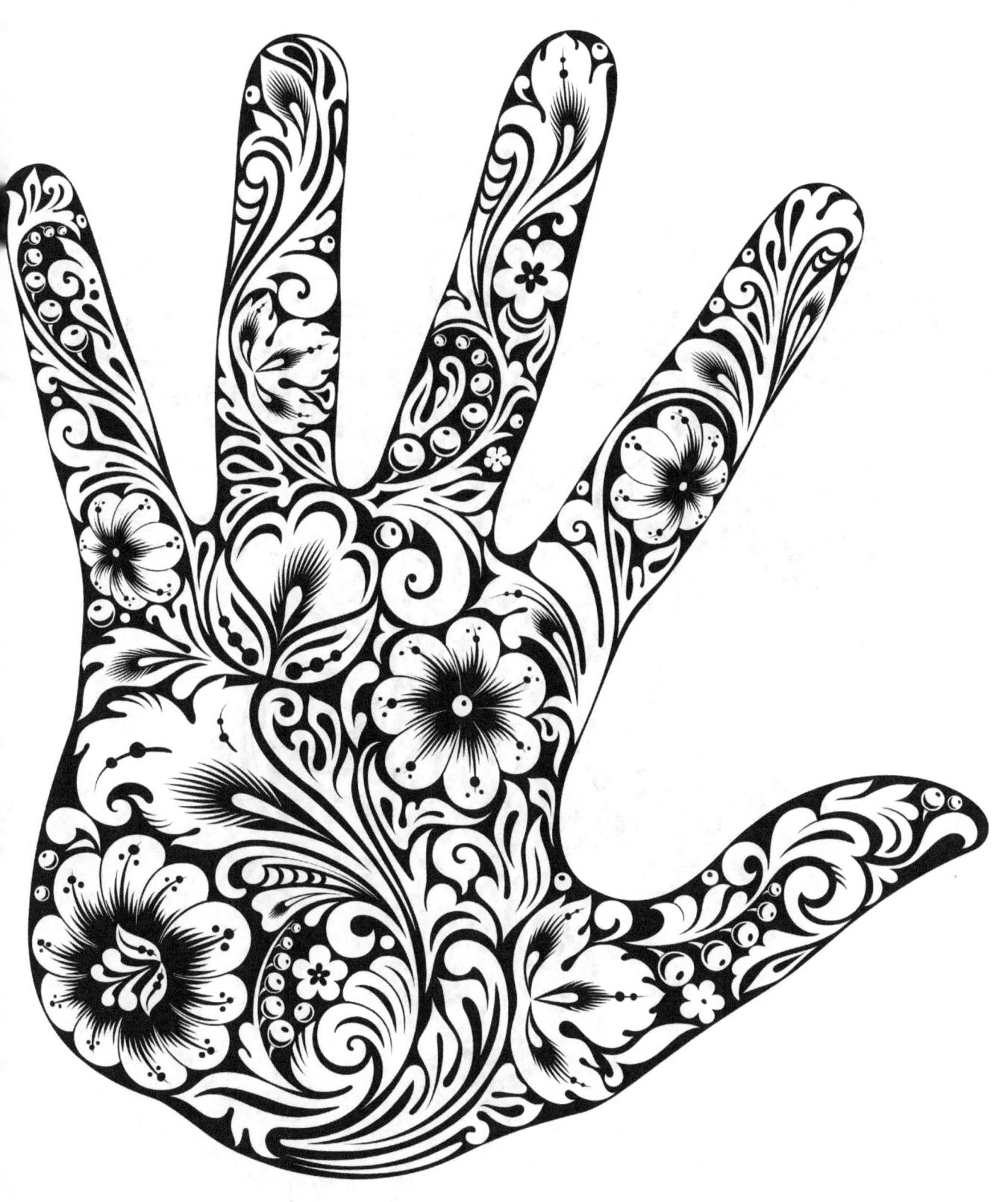

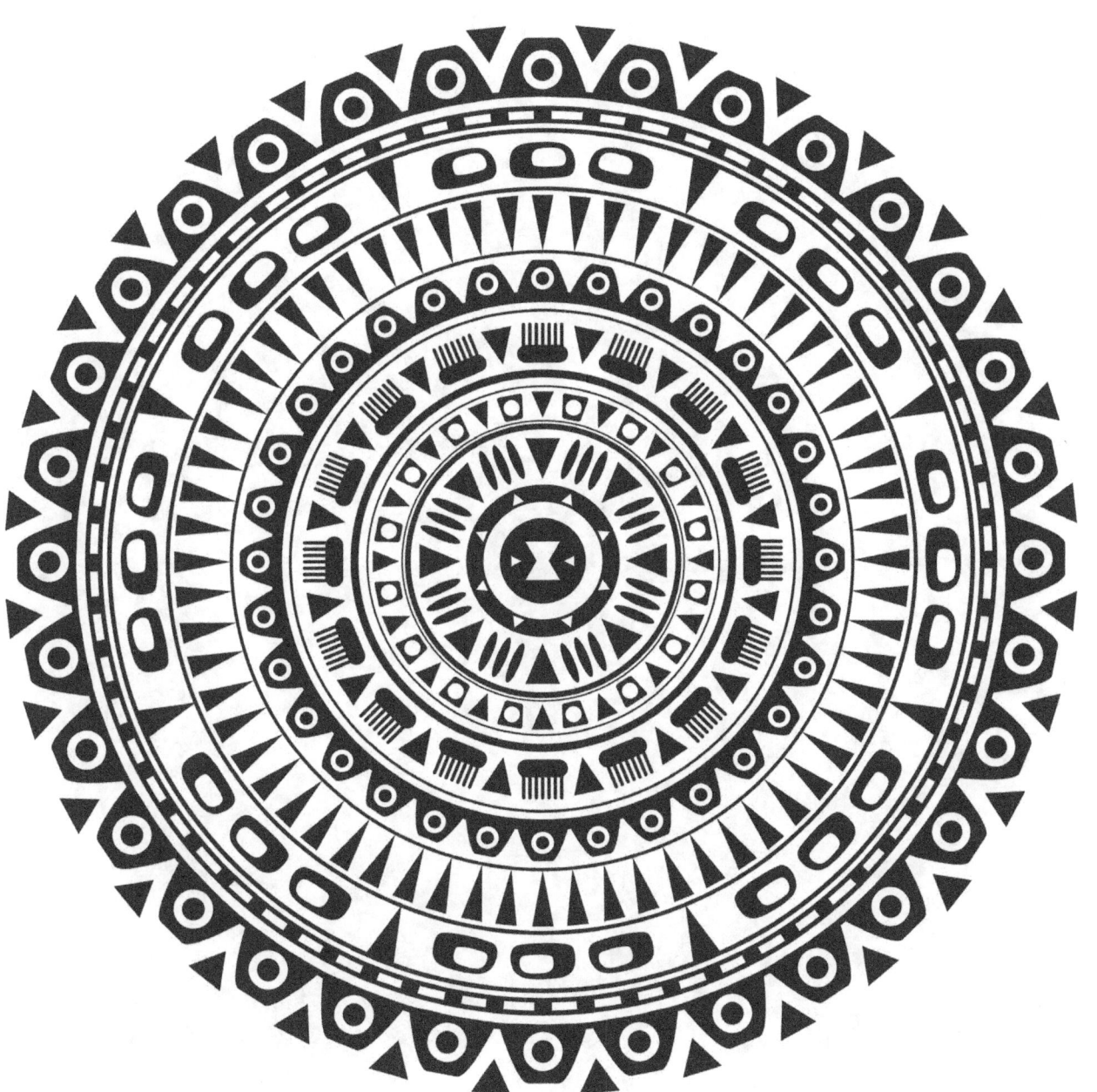

www.ingramcontent.com/pod-product-compliance
Lightning Source LLC
Chambersburg PA
CBHW081018170526
45158CB00010B/3094